CRITICAL HISTORY

AND

BIBLICAL FAITH

NEW TESTAMENT PERSPECTIVES

Edited by

Thomas J. Ryan

The Annual Publication of the

College Theology Society

The College Theology Society

Horizons

Villanova University

Villanova, Pennsylvania 19085

COLLEGE THEOLOGY SOCIETY

ANNUAL PUBLICATION SERIES

CRITICAL HISTORY AND BIBLICAL FAITH

NEW TESTAMENT PERSPECTIVES

edited by

Thomas J. Ryan

1SBN 0-933392-00-1

Distributed by College Theology Society
c/o Horizons
Villanova University
Villanova, Pa. 19085

Printed in the United States of America

Edward Brothers, Inc.
Ann Arbor, Michigan 48104

CRITICAL HISTORY

AND

BIBLICAL FAITH

NEW TESTAMENT PERSPECTIVES

Contents

Introduction

The question of the relationship of history to faith
is as ancient as Christianity itself, since Christian faith
is by its definition faith in Jesus as the Christ. The
problem begins with the very name of Jesus, since it is
the name of an historical figure from the Galilee region
of Palestine, as distinguished from the title "Christ"
which is a faith expression referring to the one appointed
by God for mankind's salvation. Any critical examination
of the equation of the name Jesus with the Christ title
accorded this historical figure by his followers is ren-
dered complex by the very nature of the primary sources
left us by those first century Christians, since these
documents are essentially creedal documents, whether letters, treatises or that uniquely Christian literary inven-
tion, the gospel. The gospels, particularly the synoptic
gospels, are unique in their conscious weaving together
of history and myth, whether that myth be archetypal
(establishing the basic psychic orientation of the Christian group) or foundational (providing the structure for
Christian identity, cohesion and way of life). Since the
Enlightenment, with the emergence of critical history, the
documents of the New Testament, particularly the gospels,
have been the source and not seldom the battleground for
exploring the relationship between history and faith.

Thus, the question of the history/faith relationship
is perennial, one that naturally surfaces when any group
of theologians and educators gathers to discuss the New
Testament. Such a group did gather at the 24th annual
meeting of the College Theology Society, held in 1977 at
St. Mary's College in Notre Dame, Indiana. Several central issues in contemporary New Testament research were
discussed, and the essays in this volume furnish a

sampling of that discussion. Six of the eight essays were
actually presented at St. Mary's.

Two considerations motivate the positioning of the
essays by Meeks and Fiorenza, which are concerned with the
social history of early Christianity, in the first part of
this volume. The first is the editor's acceptance of that
basic premise enunciated in the opening sentence of Bultmann's *Theology of the New Testament* that the historical
Jesus is the presupposition for, rather than part of, the
theology of the New Testament. The second reason has to
dc with the content of the essays themselves, which more
so than the others, advance historical methodological concepts now considered vital for contemporary and future New
Testament studies. Meeks considers the attempt to understand both the social forms of the early Christian group-
ings as well as the network of relationships between them
and the larger societies in which they functioned to be
of paramount significance for an accurate picture of first-
century Christianity. Fiorenza also is convinced that a
non-patriarchal investigation of the social history revealed
in the New Testament documents will not only provide the
basis for the reconstruction of first-century Christianity's
history according to an egalitarian model truly representative of the actual situation, but will also show that understanding the role of women in the early church is at the
center of an accurate picture of first century Christianity.

The challenge of critical history to the systematic
theologian as that history probes deeply and at times uncom-
fortably the scandal of the death-resurrection, baptism and
birth of Jesus is Mackey's concern in his essay which sets
the stage in the second part of this volume for further
reflections on the resurrection and the passion of Jesus
by Fuller, Kelly and Sloyan. This collection of essays

concludes with two articles that have a bearing on the past and the future, one in which Misner attempts in a sense to rehabilitate the places of Söderblom and Tyrell in what may be described as the older quest for the historical Jesus, and the other in which Daly explores the possibilities that contemporary biblical, historical and systematic studies offer for a Christian biblical ethic.

The publication of this volume is reflective in large measure of the quality of academic concern and leadership given the College Theology Society by its Board of Directors and particularly by its officers, James W. Flanagan, of the University of Montana, President; Jeremy Miller OP of Emory University, Vice President; Dolores Greeley RSM of St. Louis University, Secretary. At the same time, the editor takes this opportunity to express his own profound personal gratitude and that of the Society to Thomas M. McFadden of St. Joseph's College (Philadelphia), Chairman of the Publications Committee for his friendship, advice and foresight. Most helpful in preparing this volume also were Philadelphia colleagues, Professors David P. Efroymson of La Salle College, Bernard P. Prusak of Villanova University, and Gerard S. Sloyan of Temple University.

In this undertaking as in so many others, the editor owes very much to the bedrock confidence and celtic wit of his wife, Eileen.

Thomas J. Ryan
Saint Joseph's College
Philadelphia

FAITH AND THE SOCIAL HISTORY

OF EARLY CHURCH

"SINCE THEN YOU WOULD NEED TO GO OUT OF THE WORLD": Group Boundaries in Pauline Christianity

Wayne A. Meeks

In the final chapter of his remarkable book *Roman Social Relations*, Ramsay MacMullen contemplates Caesar on the verge of the Rubicon. The conventional Roman historian, MacMullen observes, understands Caesar and his immediate retinue pretty well--that is, the senate and the equestrian class. But Caesar, as he makes his decision, must understand much more: "If he leads, what follows?" The network of relationships which connect senators and *equites* with the other ninety-nine percent of the population will shape what follows, yet modern historians have barely studied it at all. "Without such study," remarks MacMullen, "we know only Caesar and his horse" (122).

Modern study of Christianity's first century is in a similar plight. The sheer quantity of intellectual industry which, even since the Enlightenment, has been concentrated on the approximately six hundred small pages of Greek that make up the New Testament is unparalleled for any other body of literature in our cultural history. Yet the focus of that industry has been astoundingly narrow. We have hardly any notion of the social forms of the early Christian groups or of the network of relationships between them and the larger societies within which they functioned.

Do those things matter? Do we really need to concern ourselves with the mob behind Caesar's horse or about the Corinthian Christians called "weak," who probably did not

understand Paul's letter? I think they do matter. How
much depends upon your conception of history and of Christianity. If Christianity were a religion of pure ideas,
they would not matter very much. But it is not and has not
ever been, and therefore it is not unimportant to ask,
"What was it like to become and be an ordinary Christian
in the first century?" It is a measure of the limits of
our historical critical scholarship that this simplest of
questions receives only vague and stammering replies.

The ordinary Christian did not write our texts; he
rarely appears in them explicitly. Yet they were written
in some sense *for* him, and in some ways he used them.
Since we do not meet him as an individual, we must seek to
recognize him through the collectivities to which he
belonged and to glimpse his life through the typical
occasions which are mirrored in the texts. That is why
in recent years there has been a revival of interest among
the historians of early Christianity in trying to describe
the first Christian groups in the ways that a sociologist
or an anthropologist might do.

Yet many of the models used by sociologists and anthro-
pologists seem remote from our problem, either because they
require quantities or kinds of data which are not available
from antiquity, or because they are constructed from observations of smaller, more homogeneous, and more stable
societies than those of the eastern Roman provinces. One
form of religious association, however, has seemed to a
number of scholars a peculiarly apt analogue to the pattern
of the earliest Christian groups. That form, which has
been one of the focal points for sociological theory from
Max Weber and Ernst Troeltsch down to the most recent
sociologies of religion, is the sect. Recently, for
example, Robin Scroggs has shown that the earliest

Palestinian Christian communities have all the characteristics of the sectarian movement in classical sociological
theory.[1] John Gager takes his cues instead from recent
work in social anthropology, describing all the varieties
of first-century Christianity as a "millenarian movement,"
that is, a particular variety of sect.[2] I myself, a few
years earlier, tried to show that certain patterns in the
Johannine literature of the New Testament are best understood as serving the needs of a sect which had in large
measure defined itself by the trauma of its rupture from
Judaism.[3]

These categories can have considerable heuristic power.
We must, however, learn to use them with greater precision
and discrimination. The term "sect" itself is subject to
misunderstanding. Troeltsch originally defined the sect
in contrast to the church. But sociologists who have pursued the Weberian approach of ideal types have not only
identified a growing number of intermediary types,[4] they
have also come to define the sect in contradistinction not
to the church but to the "world," that is, the dominant
society as a whole. Obviously this shift of perspective
makes the sect model more appropriate for describing
early Christianity.[5] When one or another part of early
Christianity is defined as a sect, therefore, this does
not necessarily mean that it stands over against emerging
"catholicism." Rather, we are talking about its relationship to the macrosociety.

Another problem is that the term "sect" is not specific enough to enable us to discriminate among different
kinds of early Christianity. Thus Johannine Christianity
as well as Pauline Christianity could aptly be called
"sects" in terms of their relation to the overall structure of a Greco-Roman city, but there are clearly some

important distinctions which ought to be made between
them. One recourse would be to adopt one of the more
recent and more precise systems for classifying different
kinds of sects. The most elaborate of these is the complex taxonomy developed by Brian Wilson.[6] Yet simply to
establish a checklist by which we could assign, for
instance, Pauline Christianity to one of the types and
Johannine to another, would be an enterprise of rather
limited utility. We must not suppose that we have understood the early Christians better simply by discovering
some new labels to apply to them. Instead, I think we
have a great deal of inductive work to do with out texts
first, before we proceed to classification. The analogues
from the social sciences can help us in discovering appropriate questions to ask along the way.

Brian Wilson classified religious sects in terms of
their "response to the world."[7] In what follows I shall
focus on just one of the varieties of early Christian
groups, and inquire about just one aspect of those groups'
response to the world, viz., the way they drew the line
between themselves and the society around them. We begin
with the observation that Pauline Christianity, like
other forms, required "conversion" of those who entered.[8]
Conversion is a radical process of re-socialization. It
entails strong symbolic and social boundaries separating
the group of converts from the macrosociety.[9] But if
the insulation of the group were complete, the process of
conversion would come to a halt. In groups as vigorously
expansive as Pauline Christianity, a certain tension must
exist between the desire for separation and the desire
to attract new converts. The degree of permeability of
the boundaries, the relative openness or closedness of
the group, thus becomes an important characteristic.[10]

We have effectively no external descriptions of the
Pauline groups, but are restricted to whatever information about them we can glean directly or infer from the
letters written by Paul and by the later members of his
school. Within those sources, the following kinds of
indicators combine to give us a tolerably clear picture
of the groups' boundaries: (1) special language emphasizing separation; (2) rules and rituals of purity;
(3) membership sanctions, especially the process for
excluding non-conformists; (4) the development of auton-
omous institutions; (5) reports of specific kinds of
interaction with the macrosociety.

Language of Separation

In the Pauline and deutero-Pauline letters, a variety
of terms distinguish Christians categorically from every-
body else. They are the *eklektoi* ("chosen"), the *agapētoi*
("beloved"), the *hagioi* ("holy ones"), the *adelphoi* and
adelphai ('brothers and sisters'). Even the most neutral
term used for non-Christians, *hoi exō* ("the outsiders"),[11]
makes the sense of separation unmistakable, but the outsiders are also regularly called *apistoi* ("non-believers")[12]
in contrast to the *pisteuontes,* and occasionally also
adikoi ("unrighteous," 1 Cor 6:1) and *hoi exouthenēmenoi
en tē ekklēsia* ("those despised in the church," 1 Cor 6:4).
They are characterized, as pagan society had been in Jewish
apologetic traditions, by catalogues of vices (e.g., 1 Cor
5:10; 6:9-11), which stem from the primary sin of idolatry
(Rom 1:18-32; compare Wis 13-15). The repetitive use of
this kind of language serves the process which Berger and
Luckmann call "reification," which tends toward "a total
identification of the individual with his socially assigned

typifications."[13] Members are being taught by this means
to conceive of only two classes of humanity: the sect
and outsiders. Ideally, each should think of himself in
every activity in the "reified" terms: "I am a Believer"
or "a Christian," with hostile connotations, that rein-
forces the self-stigmatization. This is a point to which
we shall return.

Where dualist language appears, it invariably implies
a negative view of the outside society, even in places
where the immediate function of the dualism is to reinforce the internal ordering of the group. In the earliest
of the extant Pauline letters a reference to the beginning
of the Christian group in Thessalonica distinguishes the
believers (*hoi pisteuontes*) from the remainder of society
as those who "turned to God from idols" (1 Thess 1:9).
This is Diaspora Jewish language, but it is immediately
reinforced in the next verse by an eschatological clause
with distinctive Christian content: "and to await his Son
from the heavens, whom he raised from the dead, Jesus who
rescues us from the wrath to come" (vs. 10). In Phillip-
pians, perhaps the latest of Paul's authentic letters, the
same note is sounded and the social consequences are candidly expressed. In contrast to those who are "enemies
of the cross of Christ" (Phil 3:18-19), Paul describes himself and his readers as those whose *politeuma* is in
heaven.[14] Here, too, there is an immediate eschatological
sanction in the context. The heavenly *politeuma* and heavenly savior correspond to a future transformation of the
bodily existence of the individual Christians as well as
their social life, when "all things" will be subjected to
Christ and God. This good apocalyptic belief is advanced
here to reinforce attitudes of loyalty and confidence within the Christian groups (3:17; 4:1).

Several recurrent patterns which evidently characterized early Christian preaching reinforce this consciousness of a radical, qualitative distinction between outsiders and insiders. For example, the "soteriological contrast pattern" reminds the Christians that "once" their
life was characterized by vices and hopelessness, "but
now" by eschatological security and a life of virtue.[15]
Gal 4:8-11 is a vivid instance of the use of this schema
to sanction a pattern of belief and practice within the
group. Formerly the Galatian Christians were "enslaved
to things which were non-gods by nature," namely the
stoicheia tou kosmou. Their life then was characterized
by "not knowing God" (vs. 8), their new life by "knowing,
rather being known by, God" (vs. 9). This again is language taken over from Judaism,[16] but Paul has placed the
Jew also within the category of the outsiders: before the
coming of Christ and faith he is "enslaved" under the Law,
as are pagans under the *stoicheia*. For Galatian Christians to accept the Judeo-Christian practices urged by
Paul's opponents would be for them to fall again into the
power sphere of the *stoicheia*. Thus Paul is attacking a
rival interpretation of Christianity by associating it
with the "outside," evil, and dangerous world from which
the Christians were "rescued" by conversion (1:4).[17] There
are a few places in the Pauline letters, all in paraenetic
contexts, where the Christians are urged sharply to separate
themselves as "children of light" from the "children of
darkness" in the rest of society--language which is best
known from the Essene writings found at Qumran.[18] But as
we shall see, the Pauline Christians did not emulate the
Qumran group's withdrawal from society.

If the sect expects the larger society to be hostile
toward it, and if society obliges by attacking the sect,

the experience is a very strong reinforcement of group boundaries. Sufferings and persecution form a complex set of notions in the Pauline and deutero-Pauline letters, and these notions are bound up with Paul's most fundamental theological and christological beliefs. But one clear function of the talk about suffering is to enhance the attitude of group solidarity by emphasizing the dangers from without. The paraenetic reminder in 1 Thess 3:3 f. shows that the instruction of new converts from the earliest times included warnings that sufferings must be expected.[19] Furthermore, the convert is given powerful models for the endurance of suffering. The apostle himself and his fellow workers have experienced great hostility and danger which Paul recites, for example, in the famous "peristasis catalogues" of the Corinthian correspondence.[20] The example of other Christian congregations can also be cited, as in 1 Thess 2:14. All these are related finally to the comprehensive image of Christ's sufferings and death. What other fate could believers expect so long as they live in the world that crucified the Son of God? The common paraenetic motif of "imitation" permits Paul to link the various models together: "You became imitators both of us and of the Lord, by receiving the word in great affliction with joy (inspired by) the Holy Spirit, so that you (in turn) became a model [typon] for all the believers in Macedonia and in Achaia" (1 Thess 1:6; cf. 2:14). The result is a series of structurally analogous examples, which combine to present a compelling picture of a world hostile to God's intentions and to his chosen agents. When the convert does eventually experience hostility, even in the mildest forms, perhaps from relatives, this is readily understood as confirming the sect's picture of "the way the world is."

The picture may be further reinforced by two mythic elements. The anti-divine opposition may be said to be instigated by the Devil or by demonic forces (e.g., 1 Cor 2:6-8; 2 Cor 4:4; Cph 6:11-18). Indeed, "the god of this world" may be pictured as one who opposes the true God (1 Cor 4:4). And this opposition can be integrated into a two-age dualism, as usual in Jewish and Christian apocalyptic. The present sufferings will yield in Jewish and Christian apocalyptic. The present sufferings will yield to future "glory" (2 Cor 4:17; Rom 8:18). There will be an eschatological recompense, when a judgment theophany will render punishment to the opponents and comfort to the afflicted faithful (2 Thess 1:3-12).[21]

One further component of the argot of the Pauline Christian groups needs to be mentioned, though an adequate discussion of it would require another paper as long as this one. That is the language of kinship, affection, and interdependence which suggests that the Pauline Christians thought of themselves as a new family. They are children of God--and of the apostle. They are brothers and sisters, they refer to one another as "beloved" and "friends." The Pauline letters are rich in emotional language: joy and rejoicing, anxiety, longing, and so on. Such language reminds us of the kind of socialization which the anthropologist Victor Turner calls "cummunitas": the intensive, personal, undifferentiated relationship which Turner finds shared by initiates in the "liminal" phase of rites of passage, but also over longer time spans by some kinds of marginal groups in more structured societies, especially by members of "millenarian" movements.[22] For our immediate topic it is only necessary to observe that this kind of intensive resocialization implies the dissolution of old primary relations. If the convert has found a new

family, his ties to his original family cannot remain
unchanged, as parents of adolescents attracted to new
religious cults today are discovering. One of the most
powerful causes for the hostility of the Roman literary
classes toward oriental cults, including Judaism and
Christianity, was precisely the fear that they would dis-
rupt households and, consequently, undermine the social
order. That fear was grounded in fact. This disruptive
tendency of conversion to Christianity was partly offset,
however, by the importance of the household itself as the
basic unit of Christian urban groups. Leadership in the
Pauline groups was often in the hands of relatively well-
to-do individuals in whose houses the church met. And
the reports, in the book of Acts, that Pauline congregations were sometimes founded by the conversion of whole
households, imply that a whole set of relationships--
for the Roman *familia* was of course much broader than our
nuclear families--was sometimes brought into the Christian community virtually intact. With the household,
then, came links to the rest of society and hierarchical
model that exerted its influence alongside the egalitarian,
"communitas" model of the new creation.[23]

Rules and Rituals of Purity

"The human body," writes Mary Douglas, "is always
treated as an image of society."[24] Where social boundaries are carefully guarded, there we may expect to find
concern about the boundaries of the body. This principle
can be readily illustrated from the functions of purity
rules in other sects of Judaism contemporary with early
Christianity. The Pharisees distinguished themselves

from the *amme ha- ares* by scrupulously observing the rules
of purity which had in biblical times applied to the priesthood in the sacred precincts of the Temple.[25]   The monas-
tic, hierocratic community at Qumran used yet more rigorous practices to assure their purity and to reinforce
their separation, already accomplished spatially by withdrawal into the wilderness, from the world of the Prince
and children of Darkness.   Bodily controls and purity
meant tight social boundaries not only for Jews of special
sectarian allegiances, however, who were thus bounded
from other, latitudinarian Jews, but also for ordinary
Jews who wished to maintain their identity in Diaspora
cities.   Philo puts their situation succinctly into his
expansion of Balaam's prophecy: "Israel cannot be harmed
by its opponents so long as it is "a people dwelling
alone" (Num 23:9), "because in virtue of the distinction
of their peculiar customs they do not mix with others to
depart from the ways of their fathers."[26]   The most important of these "peculiar customs" were circumcision,
kashrut, sabbath observance, and avoidance of civic rituals which implied recognition of pagan gods.

The Pauline school abolished circumcision of proselytes and all other rules that distinguished Jew from Gentile within the new community.   In the new era inaugurated
by the death and resurrection of Jesus the Messiah "there
is no distinction" between Jew and Gentile.   But by abandoning these rules, the Pauline Christians also gave up
one of the most effective ways by which the Jewish community maintained its identity over against the pagan
society within which it lived.   That was precisely the
practical issue at dispute between Paul and his opponents
in Galatia, which our preoccupation with his theological
and midrashic arguments has often obscured.   Would the

abolition of the symbolic boundaries between Jew and Gentile *within* the sect mean also lowering the boundaries between the sect and the world? The Pauline Christians answered this question with a significant ambivalence, which can be illustrated by two cases discussed in Pauline letters: the question of idolatry and rules for marriage and sex.

Interaction between sect members and nonChristians is directly at issue in the question posed by the Corinthian Christians, whether one is allowed to eat "meat offered to idols." The delicacy of the problem and its importance are apparent in the complex and far from univocal reply which extends over three chapters of the present form of 1 Corinthians and in the fact that Paul repeats his admonitions in a more general form in Romans 14:13-23. The rule of thumb is stated in 1 Cor 10:25-28: "Eat whatever is sold in the meatmarkets without any scruples of conscience, 'for the earth is the Lord's and its fullness'," and again, "If some unbeliever invites you to dinner and you want to go, eat everything set before you without scruples of conscience." There is, however, a limit: "But if someone says to you, 'This is sacrificial meat,' then don't eat it, for the sake of the one who calls it to your attention and of conscience--not yours but the other's." That is, Jewish purity rules are in themselves no longer valid for the Pauline congregations, and social intercourse between members of the sect and the larger society is encouraged. Only when those continued relationships with the outsiders cause particular difficulties within the sect itself are they to be curtailed, for purely internal expedient reasons, not as matters of conscience.

But Paul spends most of his argument on the latter side of the issue. It is the "building up" of the

community that is his prime concern. He seems to be
caught in some kind of dilemma which produces logical
difficulties in his assertions. For he agrees on the one
hand that "no idol exists in the world" and that "there
is no God but one" (8:4), yet he persists in using
traditional Jewish paraenesis (perhaps even an old Jewish
homily on Deuteronomy 32) against idolatry, including the
belief that the gods represented by the images are not
unreal, but *daimonioi* (chap. 10). Perhaps his position
appears most candidly in the repeated slogan of 6:12;
10:23: *panta exestin*, the slogan of "the strong" at
Corinth, with whom Paul agrees. There are no more purity
rules; "all is allowed." But he adds the limit, *all'
ou panta sympherei* (6:12; 10:23a), "Not everything is
advantageous." A Stoic moralist, with quite a different
conception of freedom, could also say that. But for Paul
what is *sympheron* is not what the individual by training
can perceive to be in rational accord with the universal
harmony. What he means is shown by his second reply to
the local slogan: *all' ou panta oikodomei*. It is what
"builds up" the community--not merely in the sense of
aggrandizing the organization and the power of the group
as a whole, but also in an individuating sense, making
accessible to all the members in their individual circumstances and different abilities and "gifts" the power of
the new ordering of reality, the new symbolic universe
of "the gospel."[27]

Gerd Theissen has shown that the issue of eating meat
is one which would divide members of the Corinthian congregations according to their social status. It was the
relatively more affluent members, "the strong," whose
business and social relationships would be sharply curtailed if the ban on "idol meat" were to be enforced,

while the poorer classes would be scarcely affected. The
issue is complicated because the affluent few are patrons
and leaders of the church in Corinth.[28] Paul finds himself pulled between a perception of "the power of the
Gospel" as fluid, innovative, boundary-crossing, abolish-
ing distinctions, and his concern for the internal life
and growth of the communities of believers, which seem
to demand the protection of strong boundaries.[29]

A similar ambivalence appears when sex is discussed.
The normal expectation in the Pauline groups was monogamous marriage; other forms of sexual relationship impaired
the "purity" of "holiness" of the group. The rule and the
worldview it represents were undoubtedly taken over from
Diaspora Judaism, for whom such holiness was seen to distinguish them from "the gentiles who do not know God"
(1 Thess 4:5). Jewish abhorrence of homosexuality and the
equation of irregular sex with idolatry were retained by
the Pauline Christians. "Flee from *porneia*" was part of
the basic instruction of converts (1 Thess 4:1-8; 1 Cor
&:1-16). The monogamous rule was reinforced by a commandment of Jesus rejecting divorce (1 Cor 7:10). All of these
rules emphasize boundaries. Moreover, for new marriages
and remarriages (which in general are discouraged), the
norm is marriage within the sect: "in the Lord" (1 Cor
7:39; cf. 9:5 "a sister as wife").[30] Among some Corinthian Christians sexual asceticism heightened even further
the difference between them and the world. Paul's
response, however, tends to undercut this function of
asceticism, even though he is himself celibate and praises
celibacy for those who have the *charisma* for it. He for-
bids asceticism within marriage (1 Cor 7:1-7), and urges
engaged "virgins" to marry if passion becomes a problem
(7:36-38). The reason for asceticism is not in order to

be "like the angels," but a pragmatic one: to devote all
one's energies to the mission (7:32-35).   In view of the
impending dissolution of the present world order, marriage
and celibacy are matters of indifference (7:29-31).   And
the rule of group endogamy must not be carried to the point
of encouraging dissolution of marriages in which one part-
ner has become a Christian.   On the contrary, the sphere
of the sacred is extended to the spouse and children of
such marriages, and may be the means by which they also
will be "saved" (7:12-16).

In matters of food and sex, then, the rules of the
Pauline communities seem frought with ambivalence.   Purity
and holiness of the body, both the individual body and the
metaphorical "body of Christ," are emphasized.   Yet Paul,
agreeing in this particular with "the strong" in Corinth,
does not want to draw the logical consequence that this
purity entails rigorous separation from the larger society.
The directive "not to mix" with sinners applies only within the community, not to those "of this world," for "then
you would need to go out of the world" (1 Cor 5:9-10).
Marriages with pagan partners are to be kept intact if
possible, and the ordinary social intercourse around meals
with pagans is also to continue so long as it does not dis-
rupt internal peace.

Membership Sanctions

The strength of the group's boundaries comes vividly
to expression in the fact that one of the strongest pen-
alties against violation of the group ethos is simply
exclusion, especially from common meals.   In Paul's first
attested, but not surviving, letter to the Corinthians,
he warned them "not to mingle" with anyone practicing any

one of the catalogue of typical vices, "nor to eat with
such a one" (1 Cor 5:11). The same sanction is applied
in 2 Thess 3:6-14,[32] and a formal reminder of this sanction was probably included in the eucharistic liturgy
(1 Cor 16:22 compared with Did 10:6). The penalty of
exclusion from common meals is often compared with the
regulations of the Qumran community,[33] but of course this
kind of sanction could not have the power in an urban
setting that was possible in a physically isolated sect
like the Qumran group. And the Pauline Christians lacked
also the double sanction of the Essenes that food obtained
outside the sect was "impure."[34] Nevertheless, formal
ejection from the sect could include a curse solemnly
"delivering" the transgressor into the power of Satan,
"for destruction of the flesh" (1 Cor 5:5).[35] The implication, as J. C. Hurd observes, is that the Corinthians
conceived of their group as "an island of life in Christ
surrounded by a sea of death ruled by Satan"[36]--though
Paul takes pains in the immediate context of this order
to limit that implication (5:10). Later, in both Pauline
and Johannine communities, isolation was used to enforce
doctrinal uniformity as well as moral practice (Tit 3:10;
2 Jn 10).

Autonomous Institutions [31]

The isolation of the group would be forwarded by
creating institutions to perform services for the members
for which they would ordinarily have relied upon municipal
or other "outside" organizations. The communal meals just
mentioned would be one example, since for many members,
especially of the humbler classes, the Christian assemblies

and meals provided a more than adequate substitute both
physically and socially for benefits which those persons
might otherwise have obtained from membership in *collegia*
of various sorts or from the various municipal festivals.[37]
A still clearer example comes in the admonitions of 1 Cor
6:1-11. The inescapable implication of vss. 2-5 is that
Paul expects the church to set up internal procedures to
judge civil disputes between Christians, with selected
sophoi among them acting as arbiters. The fact that the
second half of the passage (vss. 6-11) chides them for
having suits at all and urges an other-regarding ethic
which would eliminate such competition, does not remove
the practical directive. The Christians, as those destined eschatologically to share in the judgment of the
whole world, of men as well as angels, are surely compe-
tent to set up a panel to arbitrate *biōtika pragmata*
among themselves. They must not perpetrate the absurdity
of letting outsiders (*adikoi, apistoi, exouthenēmenoi en
tē ekklēsia*) decide internal conflicts.

Sanctioned Interaction with the Macrosociety

I have already mentioned the cases of marriages with
pagan spouses and Paul's encouragement of continued social
intercourse with pagans in the controversy over meat
"sacrificed to idols." The encouragement of openness
toward the world in these instances has as its primary
aim the expansion and self-defense of the church. That is
stated candidly in the case of marriages with pagans
(1Cor 7:16). Further, the ordering of the internal life
of the sect is done not in complete isolation, but with
an eye toward the way outsiders will perceive them. The

artisan ethic of *hesycheia* supported by hard work and
minding one's own business is in order to "walk decently
toward those outside" (1 Thess 4:11 f.). Ecstatic demon-
strations in assemblies of the church are to be curbed
lest unbelievers coming in (they are thus assumed to have
free access to these meetings!) should think the Christians insane (1 Cor 14:23).

The same pattern persists in the later letters of
the Pauline school. The internal life of the community
is to be conducted with a view to *tous exō* (Col 4:5), and
its basic structure, that of the *familia* or *oikia*, is the
hierarchically ordered household fundamental to all Greco-
Roman society. Emphasis upon that order, by means of the
so-called *Haustafel* which Christianity took over from the
Hellenistic synagogue, serves as a defense against the
typical objection which, as noted above, Greco-Roman
writers urged against novel cults: that they corrupt
households and hence threaten the basis of the whole
social order.[39]

In only one passage in the authentic Pauline letters
is attention directed to the political authorities; the
Christian groups' interactions and difficulties with the
larger society seem to have been primarily, at this early
stage, through the less formal social structures. It is
commonly acknowledged that in Rom 13:1-7 Paul is using a
form of paraenesis which had been formulated by the Diaspora Jewish communities. The *exousiai* to which Christians are urged here to be submissive are without doubt
the functionaries of the imperial government rather than
the municipal magistracies. Jews in the provincial
cities habitually depended upon good relations with the
imperial court and its officers, frequently for protection against local opposition. The picture of the state

is of course idealized in this context, but the experience
of the urban Jews on numerous occasions vindicated the
advocacy of this ideal as their best policy, and the
Pauline Christians followed their example. It is significant that the dualistic language which the Pauline groups
did use in their paraenesis (e.g., later in this same chapter, Rom 13:11-14) is *not* applied to the Roman power. The
demonic *archontes* are not identified as the real power
behind the human ones, as they were in the Qumran sect's
ideology and also in the New Testament Apocalypse (Rev
13 *et passim*).

In the letters we see Paul and his followers wrestling
with a fundamental ambiguity in their conception of the
social character of the church. On the one hand, it is
formed as an eschatological sect, with a strong sense of
group boundaries, reinforced by images of a dualistic
tendency and by foundation stories of a crucified Messiah
raised from the dead as the root symbol of the way God's
action in the world is to be perceived and followed.
On the other hand, it is an open sect, concerned not to
offend "those outside" but to attract them to its message
and if possible to its membership. It has other forms of
self-description and basic symbols which point toward
universality and comprehensiveness: it is the people of
the one God, including both Jew and Gentile. Indeed,
Christ is the "last Adam," the "new *anthropos*," the image
of God and therefore the restoration of humanity to its
created unity.

Did the Pauline groups together constitute a "sect"?
Or were there already in their response to the world the
seeds of the more latitudinarian form of religious socialization which the classical sociologists would call
"church"? Considering the single factor of group

boundaries, I think we should have to say that there was a powerful tension between the two directions. Paul and his fellow-workers struggled to hold together what Mary Douglas might call a simultaneously "high grid"[40] and "strong group" social environment: an inherently unstable combination, but an enormously creative one.

Notes

[1]"The Earliest Christian Communities as Sectarian Movement," in J. Neusner (ed.), *Christianity, Judaism and Other Greco-Roman Cults* (Leiden: Brill, 1975), Part 2, pp. 1-23.

[2]*Kingdom and Community: The Social World of Early Christianity* (Englewood Cliffs: Prentice-Hall, 1975), chap. 2.

[3]"The Man from Heaven in Johannine Sectarianism," *JBL* 91 (1972), pp. 44-72.

[4]An excellent survey of the history of research in this area is in Michael Hill, *A Sociology of Religion* (New York: Basic Books, 1972), chaps. 3 and 4.

[5]Cf. Scroggs, *op. cit.*, 2 f, n. 4.

[6]*Sect and Society* (London: Heinemann, 1961), and *Magic and the Millennium* (London: Heinemann, 1973).

[7]*Magic and the Millennium*, p. 21.

[8]This does not imply that they are automatically to be assigned to Wilson's "conversionist" type. Pauline Christianity will be seen to share characteristics with more than one of Wilson's ideal types. I have in mind rather A. D. Nock's classic study of religious change in antiquity, *Conversion* (Oxford: University Press, 1933), in which he distinguishes the "conversion" expected by Christianity, Judaism, and a few philosophical schools from the mere "adhesion" demanded by most of the initiatory cults of the Greco-Roman world.

[9]Peter Berger, "The Sociological Study of Sectarianism," *Social Research* 21 (1954), pp. 482-83.

[10]Compare the much wider-ranging comments of J. Z. Smith on "closed" vs. "open" or "locative" vs. "utopian" responses to the world in "A Place on which to stand," *Worship* 44 (1970), pp. 457-74, esp. p. 471; and "The Wobbling Pivot," *JR* 52 (1972), pp. 134-49. Also instructive are the observations of Mary Douglas, *Purity and Danger* (Harmondsworth: Penguin, 1970) and *Natural Symbols* (2d ed., London: Barrie & Jenkins, 1973), to which I shall return further below.

[11]1 Cor 5:12, 13; 1 Thess 4:12; Col 4:5. *Idorēs* in Cor 14:23 f. is probably an equivalent.

[12]1 Cor 6:6; 7:12-15; 10:27; 14:22-24; 2 Cor 4:4; 6-14.

[13]Peter Berger and Thomas Luckmann, *The Social Construction of Reality* (Garden City: Doubleday, 1967), p. 91.

[14]The language invites comparison with the arrangement which Diaspora Jews worked out in most Greco-Roman cities, by which, though they did not enjoy citizenship (*politeia*), they did possess a certain autonomy as a recognized *politeuma*. In contrast, Paul uses this term with an entirely transcendent referent. There is no governing structure of the Christians in Phillippi which would be recognized by the Romans, nor is there any hint that Paul imagines that such would be desirable even if possible.

[15]Eph 2:11-22; 5:8; Gal 4:8-9; cf. 3:23 ff.; Rom 6:17-22; 7:5-6; 11:30; 1 Pet 2:10; Col 1:21 f.; Eph 2:1-10; Tit 3:3-7; cf. Gal 4:3 ff.; Col 2:13 f.; 1 Pet 1:14 ff. See N. A. Dahl, "Formgeschichtliche Beobachtungen zur Christusverkündigung in der Gemeindepredigt," in *Neutestamentliche Studien für R. Bultmann* (BZNW 21; Berlin: Töpelmann, 1957), pp. 5 f. (ET: *Jesus in the Memory of the Early Church*

[Minneapolis: Augsburg, 1976], pp. 33 f.

[16]Cf. 1 Thess 4:5 *ta ethnē ta mē eidota ton theon* and 2 Thess 1:8. The phrase is probably derived from Ps 78:6 LXX; cf. Jer 10:25; Isa 55:5. See R. Aus, *Comfort in Judgment* (Diss. Yale, 1971), pp. 85-88.

[17]Gal 1:4 belongs to another well-represented type of early Christian preaching, "the teleological pattern" (Dahl,*op. cit.*, p. 7, ET, 35 f.). The *purpose* of Christ's self-sacrifice is here said to be *hopos exeletai hemas ek tou aiōnos tou enestōtos ponērou*. In the other formulae of this type, such sharp dualism does not appear directly, but those which define the purpose of the salvific action as "purification" or "sanctification" of the believers imply a similar view of the macrosociety as impure and profane (e.g., Eph 5:25b-26). But the aim of salvation can also be formulated in more positive terms, probably shaped by the traditional hellenistic synagogue propaganda, of the "new people" or equivalent expressions; e.g., Tit 2:14; cf. Barnabas 5:7 and Ignatius' letter to Smyrna 1:2, which may echo distinctively Pauline tradition as in New Testament Eph 2:12-22.

[18]1 Thess 5:4-11; Eph 5:7-14; 2 Cor 6:14-7:1. The last is commonly regarded as an interpolation, though it would have to have been added before the extended circulation of the Pauline letters, since no manuscript authority exists for omission.

[19]In time of actual persecution, Timothy has been sent to remind the congregation that, "when we are with you, we told you beforehand that we were to suffer affliction" (3:4 RSV). Compare the warnings to Jewish proselytes, which probably date from the time of Hadrian, bYeb 47a. Cf. David Hill, "On Suffering and Baptism in 1 Peter,"

NovT 18 (1976), pp. 181-89, who takes up and modifies E. Selwyn's notion of a "persecution torah" in early baptismal paraenesis.

[20]1 Cor 4:11-13; 2 Cor 4:8-12; 6:4-10; 11:23-29.

[21]We also see in 1 Thess 4:13-18 how the experience of natural death of members of the group can be turned into an occasion for extending the beliefs in parousia and resurrection to strengthen the sense of solidarity within the group. The solidarity is to be eternal: "Thus we shall always be with the Lord" (vs. 17). Note the juxtaposition in 5:1-11 of apocalyptic, dualistic terminology for the same purpose.

[22]*The Ritual Process* (London: Routledge & Kegan Paul, 1969), chap. 3.

[23]I hope to discuss this set of questions more fully at another time. For the importance of the household, see F. Filson, "The Significance of the Early House Churches," *JBL* 58 (1939), pp. 109-12; E. A. Judge, *The Social Pattern of Christian Groups in the First Century* (London: Tyndale, 1960), chap. 3; G. Theissen, "Soziale Schichtung in der korinthischen Gemeinde," *ZNW* 65 (1974), pp. 246-50. For pagan fears of disruption of the household and thence the *politeia,* and Jewish and Christian apologetic emphasis on their hierarchical household, see David Balch, *"Let Wives Be Submissive": The Origin, Form, and Apologetic Function of the Household Duty Code (Haustafel in I Peter* (Diss. Yale, 1974).

[24]*Natural Symbols,* p. 98.

[25]J. Neusner, *Rabbinic Traditions about the Pharisees before 70* (Leiden: Brill, 1971), 3 vols; summary: 3.301-19; *From Politics to Piety* (Englewood Cliffs: Prentice-Hall, 1973).

[26]*Mos.* 1.278, trans. F. H. Colson (Loeb ed.).

[27]On this concept of authority as the interpretation and mediation of power for the community, see J. H. Schultz, *Paul and the Anatomy of Apostolic Authority* (Society for New Testament Studies Monograph Series 26; Cambridge: University Press, 1975), and compare K. Burridge's description of the prophet's function in millenarian movements, *New Heaven, New Earth* (New York: Schocken, 1969), chap. 11.

[28]G. Theissen, *art. cit.*, and "Die Starkeund Schwachen in Korinth," *EvTheol* 35 (1975), pp. 155-72.

[29]The perceptive reader will recognize here the dimensions of social environment which Mary Douglas calls "grid" and "group." I hope on another occasion to apply her analytic scheme more systematically to some of the characteristics of the Pauline groups.

[30]Very likely the original use of the interpolated admonitions 2 Cor 6:14-7:1 was to discourage marriage with unbelievers (*heterozugountes apistois*), though it serves quite a different function in its present context.

[31]My discussion of this topic can be brief, because it has been the subject of a monograph by Göran Forkman, *The Limits of the Religious Community: Expulsion from the Religious Community within the Qumran Sect, within Rabbinic Judaism, and within Primitive Christianity* (CB, NT Ser. 5; Lund: Gleerup, 1972).

[32]Note the use in vs. 14 of the same verb as in 1 Cor 5:11, *me synanamignusthai*--the same verb used by Philo in *Mos.* 1.278, cited above, n.26.

[33]1 QS 6:24-7:25; cf. E. Best, *The First and Second*

Epistles to the Thessalonians (Black New Testament Commentaries; London: Black, 1972), p. 343.

[34]Josephus, *Jewish Wars* 2.8.143 f., says that some banned sectaries actually came near starvation.

[35]See G. W. H. Lampe, "Church Discipline and the Interpretation of the Epistles to the Corinthians," in *Christian History and Interpretation: Studies Presented to John Knox,* ed. W. D. Davies et al. (Cambridge: University Press, 1967), pp. 337-61; Forkman, pp. 139-51.

[36]*The Origin of 1 Corinthians* (New York: Seabury, 1965), p. 285.

[37]Cf. Theissen, "Die Starken und Schwachen," *art. cit.,* p. 164.

[38]An interesting parallel is found in an association of Iobacchoi (2d cent. A.D.) who were obliged to refer controversies to a court of honor within the group rather than a state court (F. Poland, *Geschichte des griechischen Vereinwesen* [Leipzig: Teubner, 1909], p. 501).

[39]See Balch, *op. cit.*

[40]According to her most recent definition, in her 1976 Frazer Lecture, "Mistletoe," which Prof. Douglas kindly let me see in typescript. Here positive "grid" indicates increasing individuation, heightened personal articulation of classificatory possibilities and therefore increasing freedom from externally imposed classification systems. Note that this effectively reverses the valence of "grid" as used in *Natural Symbols.*

THE STUDY OF WOMEN IN EARLY CHRISTIANITY:
Some Methodological Considerations

Elizabeth Schüssler Fiorenza

> From the inauguration of the movement for
> woman's emancipation the Bible has been
> used to hold her in the 'divinely ordained
> sphere' prescribed in the Old and New Testa-
> ments. The canon and civil law; church and
> state; priests and legislators; all politi-
> cal parties and religious denominations have
> alike taught that woman was made after man,
> of man, and for man, an inferior being,
> subject to man. Creeds, codes, Scriptures
> and statutes are all based on this idea.[1]

From the outset of the women's movement the Bible
was used against women's demand for equality and has
been criticized by feminists for its patriarchal message.
The study of women in early Christianity is thus sparked
by controversy. In addition, establishment scholars do
not consider this field to be a serious object of historical-exegetical inquiry, feminists reject it as revi-
sionism serving the patriarchal religious system, and numerous Christian apologetes attempt to defend Paul, the
Bible and Christianity. Many studies of the topic therefore are of little historical-exegetical value. Simone
de Beauvoir's diagnosis of the women's movement's literature in general applies also to the study of women in
early Christianity: "If the 'woman's question' seems
trivial it is because masculine arrogance has made it a
'quarrel' and when quarreling one no longer reasons well."[2]

A cursory survey of the literature on the topic shows a scarcity of scholarly investigations and methodological sophistication. The literature appears to be oblivious of the discussion on the "historical" Jesus. Form and tradition critical studies are rare. We do not have any consensus on the tradition or historical evaluation of texts on women. For instance, does Mk 15:40 f reflect the fact that women followed Jesus in his itinerant ministry, does it reflect the situation of the early church in which women were full disciples, or does it reflect the theology of Mark? Further, with the exception of Raymond Brown's article on "Roles of Women in the Fourth Gospel,"[3] redaction critical analyses are almost completely absent. The interest of the Lukan writings in women is often pointed out but a serious redaction critical analysis placing the question in the context of other Lukan research is still missing.[4] Redaction critical studies are needed that would analyze the different theological emphases of the New Testament authors with respect to women's role and evaluation in different community situations. Finally, we have very little research done on women in different counter-cultural movements or sectarian communities of the time which by analogy would illuminate the social possibilities of the early Christian communities. Do we find religious communities and small groups in antiquity that accord women equal status?[5] This lack of serious historical-critical analyses is in my opinion due on the one hand to the scholarly disinterest of male exegetes and historians, and on the other hand to the revisionist apologetics that motivates most studies on women in early Christianity.

Androcentric Scholarly Perspective

Thus in many exegetical and theological circles the study

of women in the Bible is not a serious and substantive
objective of exegetical and historical scholarship. Since
it is sparked by the women's movement in society and
church, it is considered to be a "fad" and not a genuine
historical-theological topic. The issue is ideologically
slanted and anyone identified with the feminist cause is
no longer considered to be a "serious" scholar. One of
my colleagues remarked about a professor who wrote a
rather moderate article on women in the Old Testament,
"It is a shame, she has ruined her whole scholarly career."

This verdict is pronounced not only about professional
research but also affects the study of women on the college level. Each semester I have to argue anew with the
chairman of my department that a course on "women in the
Bible" is a substantial introductory biblical course that
covers not only major biblical writings but also familiar-
izes the student with basic exegetical skills and theological themes as well as fundamental issues of historical
study and theological interpretation. If I would pro-
pose "Grace in the Bible" or "Biblical Anthropology" as
course titles, that would be fine. A course description
with the title "women" in it makes the course less scholarly,
objective and theologically acceptable.

Insofar as the Bible not only documents past history
but functions as the inspired scripture for present-day
religious communities, exegetical and biblical-theological
studies are by definition "engaged." The biblical exegete
and theologian never searches solely for the historical
meaning of a passage, but always raises the issue of the
relevance or importance of the text.[6] The argument that
the study of the role of women in the New Testament is
too "engaged" or biased pertains therefore to *all* biblical
inquiry and not just to the study of women. Insofar as

biblical studies are "canonical studies" they are by definition conditioned by and related to their *Sitz im Leben*
in the Christian church of the past and the present. The
study of women in the New Testament is just one paradigm
for this "situatedness" of biblical studies in general.

Of course, biblical-theological studies share this
immersion in a particular cultural and societal context
with historical studies in general which also cannot
abstract from the presuppositions, ideologies and power
structures that influence the questions and the models
within which they assemble their data. The hermeneutical
discussion [7] that has taken place in various branches of
the humanities over the past fifty years has questioned
the positivist understanding of reality and has shown
that a historicist, objectivistic historiography is impossible. The understanding of history is never determined
solely by so-called historical facts or data but always by
the presuppositions and interests of historians whose questions and methodological approaches are always decisively
influenced by social mythologies and personal experiences.
History and historiography are a selective view of the
past whose scope is not only limited by extant sources
and materials but also defined by the interests and perspectives of the present. [8] As historians perceive shifts
in the present societal-cultural fabric, they (consciously
or not) alter their presuppositions, perceptions and selections of what was important in the past and what is worth-
while studying today.

Feminist scholars rightly point out that the biblical
materials are studied by historians who consciously or
unconsciously understand them from a patriarchal perspective. [9] Scholars not only translate biblical texts in
sexist language, but also decide textual-critical questions

from a male point of view. They not only neglect to illuminate feminine imagery and symbols in the Bible but also
assume that all biblical authors were of male gender.[10]
Academic discussions about church order, discipleship,
worship, or mission in the New Testament generally presuppose that the primitive Christian church had an all
male leadership. Most investigations of the place of
women in the biblical traditions appear to share the same
cultural presuppositions. Insofar as they single out the
"role of women" in the Bible as a special problem, they
reflect our own cultural and historical perspective,
according to which male existence is the standard expression of human existence, human society, and human history.
In such a perspective only the role of woman becomes a
special psychological, societal and historical problem,
whereas the role of man and the patriarchal societal and
ecclesial structures remain unexamined. While we have
numerous studies of "women" in the Bible or early Christianity, no study exists to my knowledge of men qua men
in biblical times and of the patriarchal aspects of New
Testament theology. The fact is that maleness is the
norm of being human and being Christian.

Revisionist Apologetics

If the hermeneutical discussion has proven that we are
always "engaged" when asking historical questions, we cannot pretend that we approach the study of women in early
Christianity as "objective" historians, detached from the
interests of theology or academia, who try to give as
realistic an account as possible. Moreover, as a woman
involved in the academic study of early Christianity I

cannot afford such a stance, since the church as well as academic theology are patriarchal institutions that define "what is realistic" from a decidedly androcentric perspective. The question of theological meaning is unavoidable.

Anti-feminist preachers and writers maintained and still maintain that the submission of women and their subordinate place in family, society and church were ordained and revealed in the Bible. Whenever women protest against societal degradation and ecclesial discrimination they are referred to the Bible: Woman was created after man, she is not the image of God, she brought sin into the world, she has to be submissive, and is not allowed to speak in church or to teach men. Those upholding today the status quo which allows women to occupy only a marginal and subsidiary role in a male society and church argue on biblical grounds that women and men are essentially different and therefore must have different roles in society and church.[11] This "dual nature" concept is supposedly based on creation, on the will of Christ, and on the ideas of Paul who respected this creational difference between men and women.

Against such anti-feminist argumentation, Christian writers point out that the Bible correctly interpreted supports women's rights and equality. Not the biblical message but the patriarchal interpretation of this message preaches the subjugation of women.[12] In response to the "Woman's Bible," Frances Willard summed up the hermeneutical principle of feminist apologetics, "I think that men have read their own selfish theories into the book; that theologians have not in the past sufficiently recognized the progressive quality of its revelation, nor adequately discriminated between its records as history and its principles of ethics and religion."[13]

This apologetic principle determines many contemporary studies of women in the Bible. Several authors have sought to show that the true message of the Bible, especially of the New Testament, supports women's emancipation and dignity. Since the "subordination passages" of the Pauline literature apparently contradict this affirmation, the majority of these studies concentrates on the Pauline literature. Such apologetic interpretations advance the following arguments.

First, a literalist or fundamentalist approach maintains that the biblical texts demand the subordination of women as revealed by God, but in doing so, these texts do not infringe on women's dignity. Rather, they protect women against the misunderstandings of the time. According to this argument, Christians have to uphold this revealed truth in the face of the modern heresy of egalitarianism so that women in the 21st century may receive the revealed tradition of subordination.[14] A modification of this interpretation understands the demand of subordination as a specific Christian demand that determines Christian relationships. The demand for the subordination of women is only one specific case of subordination as specific Christian attitude and life-style.[15]

A second apologetic approach seeks to formulate a "canon within the canon." This attempt can take different forms and lines of argumentation. For example, the praxis of Jesus is set over and against the praxis of the New Testament church, Jesus the feminist is played out against Paul the misogynist.[16] Another attempt declares on source-critical grounds one string of the tradition as unauthentic and therefore not normative. For instance not only do Colossians, Ephesians, Peter and the Pastoral Epistles belong to the post-Pauline tradition, but the passages on

women in 1 Cor 11:2-16 [17] and 14:33b-35 are also secondary
insertions and do not reflect Paul's theology.

These attempts to defend scripture [18] as a *villain* of
androcentric interpretation forget that not only biblical
interpreters write from a male dominance perspective; the
New Testament authors themselves do not transmit trans-
scripts of what actually happened, but present their own
androcentric interpretation and selection of early Christian traditions. Since they select and interpret traditional materials from their androcentric point of view,
we can assume that the New Testament writings only transmit
a fraction of the possibly very rich traditions on women
in early Christianity. Most of the genuine Christian
"history" is therefore probably lost.[19] The few surviving
remnants have to be recaptured not only from the bias of
contemporary interpreters, but also sifted out from the
patriarchal records of the New Testament authors themselves.

Let me give an example of what I mean by the androcentric interpretation and bias of the New Testament
authors themselves. According to all criteria of historical authenticity women were the primary witnesses of
the resurrection.[20] Yet a closer examination of the
Easter narratives already discloses the tendency to play
down the women's role as witnesses and proclaimers of
the resurrection kerygma. This tendency is especially
apparent in Luke who stresses that Peter and the eleven
were the principal witnesses of the resurrection (Lk 24:
34) and belittles the women's witness: the words of the
women seemed to the apostles "an idle tale" that they did
not believe but had to check out (Lk 24:11). Moreover,
Luke clearly limits the women's witness to the "empty
tomb" insofar as he does not mention any resurrection

appearance to them.

Contemporary exegesis shows the same tendency to suppress the significance of the women as primary witnesses of the resurrection kerygma. "The tradition that Jesus appeared first to Mary Magdalene has a good chance of being historical . . . The priority given to Peter in Paul and Luke is a priority among those who became *official* witnesses to the resurrection" (italics mine).[21] The Vatican declaration on *Women in the Ministerial Priesthood* repeats this argument in a somewhat different form: "Contrary to the Jewish mentality, which did not accord great value to the testimony of women, as Jewish Law attests, it was nevertheless women who were the first who had the privilege of seeing the risen Lord, and it was they who were charged by Jesus to take the first paschal message to the Apostles themselves(cf. Mr. 28:7-19; Kl 24:9-19; Ju 20:11-18), in order to prepare the latter to become the *official* witnesses to the resurrection."[22]

Since the early Christian writings are not only a source of truth, but also a source of patriarchal domination and androcentric repression, an apologetic and revisionist interpretation does not suffice. A hermeneutic approach which merely attempts to rescue the biblical texts from the accusation of patriarchalism and solely attempts apologetically to *understand* the early Christian writings,[23] is in danger of becoming an ineffectual reformism that confirms the patriarchal system.[24] The attempts to save the scripture from its feminist critics overlook the fact that scripture itself is already a product of androcentric interpretation. Revisionist apologetic interpretations are not sufficiently critical of the ideology of patriarchalism and therefore can be coopted.

Patriarchal, oppressive texts on the one hand and

non-androcentric, liberating texts on the other hand cannot, however, be separated according to the model of
essence and accidence. There is no essence of revelation which could be expressed in culturally and patriarchally untinged language, while the patriarchal texts of
the Bible are regarded as culturally conditioned and therefore accidental.[25] *All* early Christian writings are
culturally conditioned and formulated in a patriarchal
milieu. Biblical revelation and truth are not found in
an a-cultural essence distilled from patriarchal texts,
but are given in those texts and interpretative models
which transcend and criticize their patriarchal culture
and religion. If this is the case, then the problem with
revisionist apologetics is not its Christian or feminist
presupposition and criteria but the failure to question
the patriarchal-theological-theological framework of the
discussion. A biblical interpretation that is concerned
with the *meaning* of the early Christian writings in a post-
patriarchal society and church must maintain that solely
the non-sexist traditions of the Bible and the non-sexist
models of biblical interpretation do justice to divine
revelation.[26] Otherwise, scripture will remain a tool for
the patriarchal oppression of women and a theological
justification for the status quo.

A Non-Patriarchal Heuristic Model of Interpretation

The sociology of knowledge has pointed out that it is
important to reflect on the theoretical models by which we
assemble historical data. As any conceptualization of
early Christian history, the reflection on what it was like
to be a woman Christian in the first century depends not

only on a perceptive interpretation of the information about women supplied by the early Christian writings, but much more on the theoretical model and conceptual framework with which we formulate our questions and organize the answers found in the biblical texts.[27]

Simone de Beauvior has pointed out that our conceptual framework is determined by the understanding that "humanity is male and man defines women not in herself but as relative to him; she is not regarded as an antonomous being. He is the subject, the absolute. She is the other."[28] In her book *Man's World, Woman's Place*, Elizabeth Janeway[29] has analyzed this conceptual framework as social mythology that determines women's and men's socialization and self-understanding and justifies the present structures of power that make women to be the "weaker sex." It seems to me that this social mythology has also determined the studies on women in early Christianity.

These studies often tacitly assume that the Jesus movement in Palestine and the early Christian church was a "man's church" and therefore only the place of women becomes a problem. Because of this attitude, it is often assumed for example, that the women mentioned in the New Testament were the "helpmates" of men, that they prepared the apostles to become official witnesses of the resurrection or that they helped Paul in his missionary work. This conceptual framework has no room for the insight that women were the primary witnesses of the resurrection or that Paul had to come to terms with the women who had leadership in the missionary communities of early Christianity. The women mentioned as leading missionaries and officers in Paul's letters did not need Paul's or the Twelve's approval of "ordination." The texts indicate that women were not just "collaborators" of Paul, but that in many cases they were missionaries *before* Paul or on the same level with Paul. Paul's missionary activity was as much dependent on the ministry of these women as their ministry was a collaboration with Paul.

Yet, the question can be raised that a feminist interpretation of the New Testament is a-historical, since these writings were formulated in a patriarchal culture and church. Or as Elaine Pagels in response to Robin Scroggs cautioned: "It is really not my intention to put Paul on trial before a panel of New Testament scholars to debate whether he is 30%, 75% or 100% a feminist. After all, these are criteria that have emerged from our own present situation. To attempt simply to judge Paul by such standards seems to me anachronistic and rather a waste of time."[30] Is it sure that on historical grounds the quest for a feminist, nonpatriarchal history of early Christianity is anachronistic and projects categories back into early Christianity which are ours but not those of the first century Christians?

In my opinion, the studies of the social world of early Christianity have made a nonpatriarchal, egalitarian model of community historically plausible, for the Jesus movement in rural Palestine as well as the Christian missionary movement in the urban centers of the Greco-Roman world was counter-cultural and "sectarian."[31] Christianity was not an integrated segment of the patriarchal culture but stood over and against the dominating societal powers of the time. Just as other small groups alienated from their society, the early Christian communities were by definition egalitarian and interpersonal. They defined themselves over and against the cultural and religious establishment of the time.

The studies of the social-cultural conditions of the

nascent Christian movement in Palestine have shown that
sociologically speaking it represented a socially and
religiously deviant group similar to other sectarian groups
in the Judaism of the first century.[32] Jesus and his first
followers were not well adjusted members of their society;
they did not accept at face value its values and institutions, but were in deviation from and opposition to
them. They rejected the purity laws of Jewish religion
and attracted the outcasts of their society. In distinction to the sect of Qumran or the Pharisees, the Jesus
movement in Palestine was not an exclusive but an inclusive
group. Jesus did not call into his fellowship righteous,
pious, and highly esteemed persons but invited tax collec-
tors, sinners and women. He promised God's kingdom not
to the rich, the established and the religious, but to
the poor, the destitute and those who did not belong.
This inclusive character of Jesus' message and movement
made it possible later to broaden the Christian group and
to invite Gentiles of all nations into the new community
which transcended Jewish as well as Greco-Roman societal
and religious boundaries.

It is debated whether the radicalism of the Jesus
movement in Palestine was assimilated by the urban Hellenistic congregations into a family-style "love-patriarchalism in which the social distinctions survived in a softened, milder form."[33] Yet, it is questionable whether
the instructions to the household members in the post-
Pauline literature can be adduced to establish such a
"love-patriarchalism" also for the initial state of the
early Christian movement in the Hellenistic urban centers.
Egalitarian models of community organization are found in
collegia or cult associations of the time which accorded
women and slaves equal standing.[34] The references of the

Pauline letters to the leadership of women in the early
Christian communities suggest that the subordination-
demands of the Christian "love-patriarchalism" were not
yet operative in the urban Hellenistic congregations before
Paul.

The egalitarian theological self-understanding of the
early Christians is expressed in Gal 3:28. In the new
community all distinctions of race, religion, class, and
gender are abolished. All are equal and one in Christ.
Exegetes more and more agree that Gal 3:28 is a traditional
baptismal formula[35] which was quoted by Paul in order to
support his view that there is no longer any distinction
between Jew and Gentile in the Christian community. This
baptismal formula expresses the self-understanding of the
newly initiated Christians over and against the religious
views of the Greco-Roman culture. It was a rhetorical
commonplace that Hellenistic man had to be grateful that
he was born a human being and not a beast, a man and not
a woman, a Greek and not a barbarian. This pattern was
adopted by Judaism and found its way into the synagogue
liturgy: three times daily the Jew thanked God that He
did not make him a Gentile, a woman, or a slave.[36]

Over and against this cultural-societal pattern shared
by Hellenists and Jews alike, the Christians affirmed at
their baptism that all political-societal differences
were abolished in Jesus Christ. It is important to note,
however, that this baptismal formula does not yet reflect
the same notion of unification as later Gnostic writings.[37]
Whereas in various Gnostic texts woman had to become "male"
and "like man"[38] in order to become a full Christian,
Gal 3:28 does not extoll maleness as the form and standard of the new life, but Jesus Christ in whom maleness as
well as femaleness is transcended. Since "Jew and Greek"

as well as "slave and free" indicate the abolition of
societal-religious differences we can safely assume that
the same is true for the third pair "male and female."
This new self-understanding of the Christian community
eliminated all distinctions of religion, class and caste,
and thereby allowed not only Gentiles and slaves to assume
egalitarian membership and leadership in the Christian
movement but also women.   Therefore, women who were marginal persons in antiquity without much social standing
were especially attracted to the early Christian movement
in Palestine and in the Greco-Roman world.

To understand women's role in early Christianity the
following characteristics of the sectarian group appear
to be especially significant.   The sectarian group is a
voluntary association that demands a total commitment
from its members.   In such a movement not based on natural
family or kinship ties, all members have equal standing
and find love and acceptance within the community.   The
communal identity of the small group does not tolerate
social divisions and stratification.   In such small counter-
cultural and counter-religious groups women find acceptance and equality.   As "insiders" they are not set apart
from the male members of the group but all members define
themselves vis-a-vis the outside world from which they
are alienated.   These characteristics of small groups
alienated from the larger society and religion are also
found in the early Christian movement.

The following two aspects are of special significance
for the role of women in this early Christian movement.
First, the inclusive egalitarian community understood
itself in kinship terms.[39]   It is the new *communio*, the
new family that radically changes the personal ties to the
original family and questions assigned family roles.

One's primary loyalty is no longer to one's biological
family since the community has taken its place as the
locus of primary allegiance. This aspect of the egalitarian Christian *communitas* has far-reaching consequences
for understanding women's role. Women and men are no
longer defined by their family roles but by their new
allegiance to the Christian community. For example,
Prisca is most frequently mentioned before her husband
Aquila because she is not defined by her role as a wife
but is recognized because of her own outstanding missionary contribution. Junias together with Andronicus is
mentioned in Rom 16:7 not because of her status as spouse
but because the couple was "outstanding among the apostles."[40] Indeed, most women referred to in the Pauline
letters are not identified by their husbands or their
children. We do not know for instance the marital status
and family role of women like Phoebe, Mary Magdalene,
Lydia or Tryphena. That discipleship replaces old family
ties and roles is most evident in the synoptic tradition.
When Jesus' family comes to see him, according to Mark 3:31-
35, Jesus points to those gathered around him as his new
family: "Whoever does the will of God is my brother, and
sister, and mother." Mark underlines the membership of
women in this new family of the Christian community.

Secondly, since language is crucial for establishing
the boundaries of the community and for resocializing
the new members of the community, it is important to understand the function of androcentric language within the
early Christian group. The language of the small, alienated group defines its boundaries over and against the
"world" and differentiates the insiders from the outsiders
who become "the others."[41] Consequently in such counter-
cultural groups androcentric language is not employed to

delineate male boundaries and roles from those of females
or to define women as "the other."[42] Androcentric terms
are used not in a gender specific way but in an inclusive
mode meaning all members of the community in distinction
to those who are outsiders. Masculine terms as for instance
ekelektoi, hagioi, adelphoi or *hyoi* do not characterize
males as the elect, saints, brothers or sons over and
against women but these terms define *all* Christians over
and against the wider society and religion. If this is
the case, then *all* titles of the earliest New Testament
writings pertain to *all* members, male and female. Androcentric language has to be understood not as gender
specific language but as inclusive language since it pertains to an inclusive, egalitarian, counter-cultural group
or sect. We, therefore, have to assume that masculine
titles of leadership such as apostles or disciples are
also inclusive of women until proven otherwise. Rom 16:1
proves this assumption. Here the masculine form of the
title *diakonos* refers to a woman. If Paul applies this
title to himself, Apollos, Timothy, Tychicus or Epaphras,
exegetes usually render *diakonos* as minister or deacon,
whereas here they translate it with servant or deaconess
because it designates a woman, Phoebe. However, the test
does not discriminate between the office of the male and
the female *diakonos*. Such a distinction is derived from
a later time when the church had adapted to the patriarchal and hierarchical order of its Greco-Roman culture.

The gradual institutionalization and adaptation of
the early Christian movement to its patriarchal culture
destroyed the egalitarian character of the small counter-
cultural group and led to the patriarchalization of the
Christian community and its leadership functions. This
structural solidification had by necessity to eliminate

women from leadership functions within the Christian community and to relegate them to subordinate feminine roles. The progressive adaptation of the Christian movement to its patriarchal culture and the institutionalization of charismatic authority in patriarchal offices resulted in the marginalization of women. From the very beginning this patriarchalization and institutional solidification of the Christian community was opposed by egalitarian charismatic movements within the church that insisted on the full discipleship and leadership of women. However, the more the church became a genuine segment of the patriarchal Greco-Roman world, the more it had to reject such egalitarian movements. Against those groups that maintained the leadership functions of women, the patriarchally adapted church argued that women's role is that of submission and silence in church. The leadership claims of women were incorporated into the patriarchal church structures insofar as women were relegated to "feminine" roles or were marginalized in sectarian groups.

The trajectory of the Pauline tradition which stresses the subordination of women on theological grounds reflects this reactionary patriarchal evolution of the Christian community. Scholars discuss whether or not Paul himself initiated this patriarchal reaction,[43] whether it was influenced by the synagogal order, or whether it is a development of the post-Pauline school. Certainly, however, the theological justification of women's secondary role in the Christian community and of the patriarchalization of Christian leadership was very soon able to claim the authority of Paul without being challenged.

Even though 1 Cor 11:2-16 concedes to women the gift of prophecy and the performance of liturgical functions, the passage nevertheless clearly demands that women adapt

to the role definitions of their society. This demand
is theologically justified by the reference to the revealed
hierarchy "God - Christ - Man - Woman." The author argues
against an egalitarian understanding expressed in vv 11-12:
"Nevertheless, in the Lord woman is not independent of man
nor man of woman: for as woman was made from man, so man
is now born of woman. And all things are from God." He
does not intend to deny this egalitarian understanding
but maintains that the behavior of women in the congregation has to conform to the patriarchally defined customs
and roles of women. The church order in 1 Cor 14:33b-36
explicitly maintains the patriarchal order.[44] It affirms
the priority of the male insofar as it allows only him an
active participation in the worship assembly. It prohibits
women from speaking in the assembly but directs them to
their husbands for religious instruction. The *Haustafeln*
of the deutero-Pauline literature uphold the patriarchal
order of the family. These rules of conduct were univer-
sally accepted in Judaism and Hellenism and soon became
a part of Christian theology.[45] According to them women
express and practice their Christian faith and leadership
in observing the patriarchal social order.

The Pastoral Epistles provide ample proof that at the
beginning of the second century the Christian community
and its offices were perceived and patterned after the
structures of the patriarchal family. Church authority
was vested in elders, deacons and bishops. Criteria for
their election from the male members of the community
were as follows" they must be husbands of one wife and
must have demonstrated their ability to be in charge of
the community by the proper ordering of their households
and the successful upbringing of their children.[46] The
patriarchal household model which in the Greco-Roman

world was the bulwark of the political and social order now becomes *the* model of church and gradually replaces all egalitarian forms of community. This patriarchalization of the Christian community could not tolerate women in ecclesial roles of leadership. It reduced these roles to subordinate and patriarchally defined gender roles. The order of the widows and deaconesses no longer provided leadership and service for all members of the community but was mainly directed and limited to the service of women. Moreover, women's leadership in the church was no longer exercised by all women but only by those who as virgins or widows had transcended biological sex roles. In Gnostic as well as in orthodox Christian groups, Encratism and maleness became the standard of being a full Christian and disciple. According to the apocryphal Acts of the Apostles women had to renounce marriage and family in order to become Christians and missionaries. A comparison of Thecla with Prisca indicates the difference between the role of women in the early Christian movement and in the later patriarchalized Christian community. The latter had no room for women's leadership and was no longer able to subordinate family roles to those of discipleship.

Conclusion

The reconstruction of a nonpatriarchal, egalitarian model for community life in the early Christian movement as well as the recognition of its gradual patriarchalization and cultural adaptation has important consequences for the discussion of women's role in the church today. It makes clear that a patriarchal model of church by definition has to relegate women to their patriarchally defined family roles, to adapt them to the standard of maleness

as the standard of full humanness, or to marginalize them
in fringe groups. A patriarchal church has by necessity
to define women not by their Christian vocation to
discipleship but by their biological sexuality and family
relations. Only if the church and its structures shed
their patriarchal character and again become egalitarian
will women be able to participate fully and equally in
Christian discipleship and leadership.

Since the egalitarian vision of community could not
be embodied in a patriarchal church, throughout church
history women could live their vocation to full discipleship only in "sectarian" fringe groups with an egalitarian
character. The patriarchalism of the church could not
fully suppress the egalitarian traditions of the early
Christian movement and therefore repeatedly sparked so-
called heterodox movements in which women had egalitarian
standing and leadership.

> This love-patriarchalism then repeatedly moved in
> to assimilate or exclude the radical movements.
> The latter as we know occurred with more patriarchal-
> ism than love, in fact by the use of physical force
> which could have irreparably compromised Christianity
> if it had not been for the call to repentance which
> recurrently was sounded out of the traditions of
> early Christian radicalism.[47]

Today the patriarchal church is again called to repentance and conversion. It is called to abandon all forms
of sexism by rejecting a patriarchal institutional and
symbolic framework that perpetuates the inequality of
women.[48] Only the re-creation of egalitarian, nonpatriarchal communities will be able to recapture the
inclusive community of discipleship that stands at the
beginnings of the Christian movement.

Notes

[1] E. Cady Stanton, *The Original Feminist Attack on the
Bible* (*The Woman's Bible*) (New York: Arno Press, 1974),
p. 7.

[2] A. S. Rossi, *The Feminist Papers* (New York: Bantam,
1974), p. 686.

[3] R. E. Brown, "Roles of Women in the Fourth Gospel,"
Theological Studies 36 (1975), pp. 688-99; cf. also the
popular version by S. M. Schneiders, "Apostleship of Women
in John's Gospel," *Catholic Charismatic* 1 (1977), pp. 16-
20.

[4] C. F. Parvey, "The Theology and Leadership of Women
in the New Testament," in R. R. Ruether, *Religion and
Sexism* (New York: Simon & Schuster, 1974), pp. 117-49.
A short description of the passages on women in Luke and
Acts is attempted on pp. 137-46, but does not give a tra-
dition and redaction critical analysis.

[5] In the context of the Women's Studies movement there
is a recent resurgence of interest in women in antiquity.
The first major publication was a special issue of
Arethusa 6 (1973) on women in antiquity; S. B. Pomeroy,
Goddesses, Whores, Wives, and Slaves (New York: Schocken
Books, 1975) is the first comprehensive monograph on the
topic. Cf. also M. Lefkowitz, *Women in Antiquity* (Toronto:
Hakkert, 1976); Marilyn B. Arthur, "'Civilized' Women:
The Classical World," in Bridenthal/Loonz (ed.), *Becoming
Visible: Women in Eurpoean History* (Boston: Houghton
Mifflin, 1977), pp. 60-89; and her review essay "Classics,"
Signs 2 (1976), pp. 382-403; L. Goodwater, *Women in
Antiquity* (Metuchen: The Scarecrow Press, 1975) presents

an annotated bibliography. For Judaism, cf. L. Swindler, *Women in Judaism: The Status of Women in Formative Judaism* (Metuchen: Scarecrow Press, 1976).

[6]Cf. for a general discussion K. Frör, *Biblische Hermeneutik* (Müchen: Kaiser Verl., 1961) and my attempt to apply the teachings of the Constitution of Vatican II on "Divine Revelation" to the theological problem of the passages on Women in the NT: "Understanding God's Revealed Word," *Catholic Charismatic* 1 (1977), pp. 7-10; cf. also J. A. Sanders, "Hermeneutics," *Supplementary Volume: The Interpreters Dictionary of the Bible* (Nashville: Abingdon, 1976), pp. 402-07.

[7]Cf. R. Funk, *Language, Hermeneutic and Word of God* (New York: Harper & Row, 1966), pp. 1-122; W. G. Doty, *Contemporary New Testament Interpretation* (Englewood Cliffs: Prentice Hall, 1972); E. Schillebeeckx, *The Understanding of Faith* (New York, 1974).

[8]H. Smith, "Feminism and the Methodology of Women's History," in B. A. Carroll, *Liberating Women's History* (Urbana: University of Illinois Press, 1976), pp. 368-84; cf. Also K. Mannheim, *Ideology and Utopia* (London: Routledge & Kegan Paul, 1954), p. 243: "Every epoch has its fundamentally new approach and its characteristic point of view and consequently sees the 'same' objects from a new perspective."

[9]I use *"patriarchal"* to describe a societal system of male dominance and female submission. A glance at *Webster's New Collegiate Dictionary* recognizes that patriarch/patriatchal today is mostly used with respect to certain church offices (p. 840).

[10]An exception is P. Achtemeier, *Mark* (Philadelphia:

Fortress Press, 1975), p. 111: " . . . the author nowhere identifies himself (or herself); women played a prominent role in the primitive church and especially in the Gospel we are investigating, . . . so there is no certainty about the gender of the author." Cf. also A. V. Harnack, "Probabilia über die Addresse und den Verfasser des Hebraerbriefes," *ZNW* 1 (1900), pp. 16-41.

[11]Cf. "Vatican Declaration: Women in the Priesthood," *Origins* 6 (1977), pp. 518-24; Pastoral Commission of the Sacred Congregation for the Evangelization of Peoples, "The Role of Women in Evangalization," *Origins* 5 (1976), pp. 702-07, and the affirmative article by D. Burrell, "The Vatican Declaration: Another View," *America* (April 2, 1977), pp. 289-92: " . . . for I cannot but suspect that Lawrence would find the Vatican Declaration profoundly accurate in the way it links sexuality with the symbolic dynamics of human salvation." For a feminist analysis of D. H. Lawrence's understanding of sexuality as "phallic," cf. K. Millett, *Sexual Politics* (New York: Avon Books, 1971), pp. 237-93.

[12]See, for example, Phyllis Trible, "Depatriarchalization in Biblical Perspective," *JAAR* 41 (1973), pp. 30-48, as a paradigm for such attempts.

[13]E. Cady Stanton, *op. cit.*, p. 200.

[14]J. H. Yoder, *The Politics of Jesus* (Grand Rapids: Eerdmans, 1972), p. 177, n. 22.

[15]See, for example, E. Kähler, *Die Frau in den Paulinischen Briefen* (Zurich: Gotthelf Verl., 1960); V. Ramsey Mollenkott, *Women, Men & the Bible* (Abingdon: Nashville, 1977).

[16]For such popular accounts on Jesus, see, L. Sergia,

Jesus and Woman (Virginia: EPM Publications, 1975); R.
Conrad Wahlberg, *Jesus According to a Woman* (New York:
Paulist Press, 1975) and the by now famous article of
L. Swidler, "Jesus Was a Feminist," *Catholic World*, 212
(January 1971), pp. 177-83.

[17]Cf. W. Munro "Patriarch and Charismatic Community
in 'Paul'," in Plaskow/Romero, *Women and Religion*
(Missoula: Scholars Press, 1974), pp. 189-98; Wm. O.
Walker, "1 Corinthians 11:2-16 and Paul's View Regarding
Women," *JBL* 94 (1975), pp. 94-110 and the evaluation of
this attempt by J. Murphy-O'Connor, "The Non-Pauline
Character of 1 Corinthians 11:2-16?," *JBL* 95 (1976), pp.
615-21.

[18]Cf. A. Feuillet, "La dignité et le rôle de la femme
d' apreš quelques textes pauliniens," *NTS* 21 (1975), pp.
157-91; J. Massyngberde Ford, "Biblical Material Relevant
to the Ordination of Women," *JES* 19 (1973), pp. 669-94.

[19]This we have to assume if we take the results of
form criticism seriously. Therefore, the impression that
our information about women in New Testament times corresponds to the actual historical reality is misleading.

[20]Cf. M. Hengel, "Maria Magdalena und die Frauen als
Zeugen," in Betz/Hengel/Schmidt (ed.), *Abraham unser Vater*
(Leiden: Brill, 1963), pp. 243-56; and my article "Mary
Magdalene" Apostle to the Apostles," *UTS Journal* (April
1975), pp. 22 ff.

[21]R. E. Brown, *art. cit.*, p. 692, n. 12.

[22]"Vatican Declaration: The Ordination of Women,"
The Pope Speaks 22 (1977), p. 110.

[23]For a systematic account, see my article "Feminist
Theology as a Critical Theology of Liberation," *Theological*

Studies 36 (1975), pp. 605-26.

[24]M. Daly, *Beyond God the Father* (Boston: Beacon Press, 1973), pp. 4-6; cf. also G. Gutierrez, "Where Hunger is, God is not," *The Witness* (April 1977), p. 6: "Human history has been written by a white hand, a male hand, from the dominating social class. The perspective of the defeated of history is different. Attempts have been made to wipe from their minds the memory of their struggles. This is to deprive them of a source of energy, of an historical will to rebellion."

[25]Cf. also the literature on the discussion of New Testament ethics.

[26]The Declaration of Vatican II on "Divine Revelation" explicitly states the hermeneutical principle which should be applied to evaluate historically and culturally conditioned statements of the Bible. The model followed by the Constitution is not that of "essence and accidence" but that of the incarnation. Just as the Son of God became human to "save the world" (Jn 3:16), so "Scripture must be acknowledged as teaching solidly, faithfully, and without error that truth which God wanted put into the Sacred Writings *for the sake of our salvation*" (n. 11; emphasis mine). See my article, "Understanding God's Revealed Word," *op. cit.*, p. 8 f.

[27]For the heuristic value of "models," cf. I. G. Barbour, *Myth, Models and Paradigms* (New York: Harper & Row, 1974).

[28]S. De Beauvoir, *The Second Sex* (New York: A. Knowph, 1953).

[29]E. Janeway, *Man's World, Woman's Place* (New York: Dell, 1971), points out the emotional component of social

mythology and insists that not logic but only "an answer *in reality* to those needs which the myth answers in fantasy" will change such social mythology" (p. 307).

[30]E. Pagels, "Paul and Women: A Response to Recent Discussion," *JAAR* 42 (1974), p. 547.

[31]For a definition of the label "sectarian," cf. R. Scroggs, "The Earliest Christian Communities as Sectarian Movement," in J. Neusner, ed.), *Christianity, Judaism and Other Greco-Roman Cults*, II (Leiden: Brill, 1975), pp. 1-23, 1-7

[32]Cf. J. G. Gager, *Kingdom and Community: The Social World of Early Christianity* (Englewood Cliffs: Prentice Hall, 1975), pp. 22-37 and R. Scroggs, "The Earliest Christian Communities," *op. cit.*

[33]For the differentiation between the Palestinian and the missionary early Christian movements, cf. G. Theissen, "Itinerant Radicalism: The Tradition of Jesus Sayings from the Perspective of the Sociology of Literature," *Radical Religion: The Bible and Liberation* (Community for Religious Research and Education, 1976), pp. 84-93; the ET of "Soziale Schichtung in der korinthischen Gemeinde Ein Beitrag zur Soziologie des hellenistischen Urchristentums," *ZNW* 65 (1974), pp. 232-72.

[34]For the equal participation of women in cult associations, *collegia* and philosophical schools, cf. L. Swidler, "Greco-Roman Feminism and the Reception of the Gospel," in Jaspert/Mohn, *Traditio-Krisis-Renovatio aus theologische Sicht* (Marburg: Elwert Verlag, 1976), pp. 49-52; for the Isis cult, cf. S. Kelly Heyob, *The Cult of Isis among Women in the Graeco-Roman World* (Leiden: Brill, 1975), pp. 81-110; for a general characterization which does

however not pay attention to women, cf. R. L. Wilken, "Collegia, Philosophical Schools, and Theology," in Benko/ O'Rourke, *The Catacombs and the Colosseum* (Valley Forge: Judson Press, 1971), pp. 268-91.

[35]Cf. W. A. Meeks, "The Image of the Androgyne," *History of Religion* 13 (1974), pp. 165-208, 180 ff.

[36]For rabbinic passages similar to Gal 3:28, cf. J. Liepoldt, *Jesus und die Frauen* (Leipzig: Quelle & Meyer, 1921), p. 14: "Wenn ein Armer zu einem Menschen kommt und ihn anredet, hört man ihm nicht zu; auf einen Reichen hört man und nimmt ihn auf. Aber bei Gott sind alle gleich: Frauen und Sklaven, Arme und Reiche." and "Ob Israeli oder Heide, ob Mann oder Weib, ob Sklave oder Sklavin; je nach den Werken des Menschen ruht auch der heilige Geist auf ihm."

[37]This is maintained by W. A. Meeks, *op. cit.*, and R. Scroggs, "Paul and the Eschatological Woman: Revisited," *JAAR* 42 (1974), p. 536. Yet both authors appear to identify sexual distinctions and gender role distinctions. H. D. Betz, "Spirit, Freedom and Law: Paul's Message to the Galation Churches," *Svensk Exeg. Arsbok* 39 (1974), pp. 145-60 correctly emphasizes that male and female societal cultural roles are abolished.

[38]As, for example, the *Gospel of Thomas, Gospel of Mary, and Pistis Sophia.*

[39]Cf. the analysis of R. Scroggs, *art. cit.*, pp. 14 f.

[40]Cf. M. J. Lagrange, *Saint Paul. Épître aux Romains* (Paris, 1916), p. 36.

[41]Cf. the articles by R. Scroggs and W. A. Meeks cited in note 37.

[42]For the problem of androcentric language, cf. R. Lakoff, *Language and Woman's Place* (New York: Harper, 1965); Miller/Swift, *Words and Women* (Garden City: Anchor Press, 1976) and the comprehensive bibliography in M. R. Key, *Male/Female Language* (Metuchen: Scarecrow Press, 1975); G. H. Tavard, "Sexist Language in Theology," *Theological Studies* 36 (1975), pp. 700-24; L. M. Russell, "Changing Language and the Church," in *The Liberating Word* (Philadelphia: Westminster, 1976), pp. 82-98.

[43]The answer to this problem depends on whether one accepts 1 Cor 11:2-16; 14:33b-36, Colossians, Ephesians and the Pastoral Epistles as Pauline.

[44]Cf. G. Dautzsnberg, *Urchristliche Prophetie* (Stuttgart: Kohlhammer, 1975), pp. 257-73; H. W. Bartsch, *Die Antänge urchristlicher Rechtsbildungen* (Hamburg: Bergstedt 1965), p. 69.

[45]Cf. J. E. Crouch, *The Origin and Intention of the Colossian Haustafel* (Gottingen: Vandennoeck & Rupprecht, 1972), for a review.

[46]Cf. my article "Interpreting Patriarchal Traditions," in L. Russell, *op. cit.*, pp. 55-59.

[47]G. Theissen, "Ininerant Radicalism," *art. cit.*, p. 91.

[48]Cf. the understanding of conversion in B. Lonergan and my article "Feminist Theology," p. 610. Just as the Church has rejected racism and anti-Semitism it has to repudiate sexism.

HISTORY AND THE DEATH--RESURRECTION

OF JESUS

CHRISTIAN FAITH AND CRITICAL HISTORY:
The Systematician and the Exegete

James P. Mackey

"If the love of a subject can help one to understand it, it will also, I hope, be recognized that I have not been wanting in this condition. To write the history of a religion, it is necessary: firstly, to have believed it (otherwise we should not be able to understand how it has charmed and satisfied the human conscience); in the second place, to believe it no longer in an absolute manner, for absolute faith is incompatible with sincere history." The style is unquestionably that of Ernest Renan. The passage from his *Life of Jesus*,[1] one of the most delightfully artistic, if also one of the most artfully misleading lives to come from the critical period, a period of Christian source scholarship which spans two centuries, from Reimarus to the present time. The central theme of the passage states a conviction which had slowly grown during that critical period and which received its most trenchant expression in Bultmann's blunt statement that "faith, being personal decision, cannot be dependent upon a historian's labor."[2]

In contributing some introductory reflections of a systematic-christological nature to this volume, I choose to arrange my reflections around the undoubted center of two centuries of the christological problematic: the problem of our faith's relationship to history. I hope that my arrangement of title and subtitle will not be misunderstood. I do not believe that the systematician has to deal purely with faith and the exegete merely with history. The relationships between them are much more subtle and complex than that. But I do believe that up to this moment it is the exegetes who have had the most explicit effect upon the systematicians, driving them from one formed system to another, driving them out of systematics altogether, driving them sometimes into despair that any system whatever can be fashioned by anyone at this time. Most of the christologies written nowadays, for instance, are New Testament christologies. That is to say, they are either christologies written by New Testament scholars, or they are slightly selective summaries of the best New Testament scholarship available. I would suggest that the influence running between systematician and exegete should be a little more reciprocal.

The very genius of his discipline brings the exegete close to the historian, and Christians have always felt that Jesus of Nazareth, whom they name Christ, is normative for their faith. It should cause no surprise, then, that the history of the quest of the historical Jesus and the history of the development of modern critical methods of biblical interpretation lead us back to the same Reimarus and cover much the same ground along the way. Like most enterprises which boast of the critical quality, this joint onslaught on the biblical text and the person of the Founder proved most persistently self-revisionary. All of which has left the impression that we should state lightly our present conclusions about text and Founder, and has caused the systematicians in particular that feeling of near despair.

Yet, time and time again, men from many disciplines, from the great Hegel to the relatively lesser Paul Ricoeur, have warned those who deal with an historical text about how easily they may slip from reading out of it to reading into it. Here is how Hegel expressed his conviction about the incidence of eisegesis in exegesis: "The giving of the sense (of Scripture) means, however, the bringing forward of the sense into consciousness; into the region of ideas, and these ideas, which met their determinate character elsewhere, then assert their influence in the exposition of the sense supposed to be contained in the words."[3] And Paul Ricoeur explains how a text, as opposed to a spoken word, of its very nature breaks out of the intentional world of its author, finds readers and enters into a relationship which its author could not have intended and so did not intend.[4] Within the course of the modern critical study of the sources of christology, Martin Kähler, a man largely ignored until the great Bultmann took up some of his themes, had pointed out the almost equal dogmatism of the christologies of the new historical and textual critics on the one hand, and the old systematicians on the other.

Once again, though I hope I will not be misunderstood, I do not suggest that exegetes are necessarily more unaware of their presuppositions than the rest of us, or more inclined to read these into their texts. I know of their insistence on recognizing one's persuppositions before attempting to truly understand what an ancient writer wished to convey to a chosen group of long vanished readers. And I know, too, that the dominant direction in contemporary New Testament scholarship is toward the detailed discovery of the sociological, political, economic, geographical and general cultural background from which the

New Testament documents were written and against which
their original meaning can best be understood.

What, then, do I wish to suggest? Where does the
systematician enter? I had better be clear about this,
since I do fully intend to criticize, precisely as a
systematician, some common christological conclusions
found in New Testament studies today in spite of all their
historical sophistication. The systematician, when he is
not behaving like a garbage collector on the run, picking
up the throw-outs of exegetes and other historical
scholars and trying to assemble these by means of some
quick logic before something else is thrown at him, is
more akin to the philosopher than to the historian. The
systematician realizes, at his best, that all human beings
are systematicians under the skin. This is because a
system is much less the result of a static logic tying
together rather disparate topics, and much more the result
of a dynamic logic by which a single vision, a key idea,
a foundational impression of the world, moulds areas of
our human experience into a single world view. Just as
it is the philosopher's particular gift to be able to
give clear and distinct expression to the otherwise dif-
fuse mentality of a time, revealing its cognitional foundations and probing its furthest implications, so it is
the systematician's primary service to the Christian
community to detect the dominant vision, the normative
idea, the moulding impression, which is operative in any
system of Christian myth or Christian thought, to probe
its furthest implication (whether these are drawn by its
author or not), and to compare each system with others.

In order to be able to institute this comparison,
the systematician needs to be something of a historian;
in order to introduce a normative element to the comparison,

the systematician needs to know something of the faith
of the Founder. There are, of course, other ways to the
faith of the Founder besides the academic, and I shall
refer to the principal one of these later, but at the
moment I am thinking about the academic project, and so
I see clearly where the systematician needs the exegete
and I cheerfully acknowledge the enormous debt which
systematicians owe to modern biblical scholarship.

But it is also part of my intention to reinstate
the self-confidence of the systematician, to do something
to refurbish his or her image, and to reclaim the systematician's role in the contemporary quest of the historical
Jesus. Just as the Systematician needs to be something
of an historian, though that is not his primary skill,
so the exegetical-historical scholar needs to be something of a systematician in order to be able to detect
and deal with the deepest, most unconscious, and therefore
most influential of what he calls his presuppositions.
The ideal, then, since few of us are given more than one
talent to work with, is a cooperative enterprise between
systematics and exegetical-historical scholarship. In
the end, it is as much in the interest of such cooperation, as with the intent of presenting the ordinary
systematician once more in a favorable light that I offer
the following critical remarks. (The great systematicians,
of course, like Barth and Tillich, have no need of an
apologia.)

The Resurrection

In the course of his lectures to the 1977 Summer
School at the University of San Francisco, Raymond Brown
identified three christological moments, as he called them,

which are presented in the New Testament: the resurrection, the baptism and the birth of Jesus. There are
already some important (though usually unnoticed) logical
problems about placing resurrection with baptism and birth,
and these, when noticed and finally examined, can do a
great deal to reveal an exegete's basic presuppositions
in approaching the New Testament. But for the moment,
in order to restrict further my central topic of Christian faith and critical history, let me accept these
three moments and confine my comments to them.

It is a habit common to both exegetes and systematicians these days to think of the resurrection of Jesus,
if not as the event which made him Son of God, Christ,
Lord--in fairly simplistic interpretation of texts like
Acts 2:32, Acts 5:31, Acts 13:33, Rom 1:1-3--then at least
as the event which, as witnessed in the appearances to
his disciples, "revealed" this status of his and thus
enabled a faith in him to emerge which before that had
not existed at all or, though it had begun to exist, had
been destroyed by his cruel death as a convicted criminal.
Indeed, the very common tendency to speak so casually
about "before" and "after" the resurrection not only confirms the impression that we are here dealing with an
event like other events on the spatio-temporal continuum
(like birth and baptism), but strengthens the conviction
that the resurrection had a constitutive function vis-à-
vis the faith of Jesus' followers which no event of his
earthly life, and certainly not his death, could have
had. There are so many examples of this type of presupposition about the resurrection of Jesus in the New Testament that it needs no documentation. If I quote a sentence of Reginald Fuller's here, it is because the senti-
ment he expresses is so common; the sentence itself
traces its content at least to Dibelius: "Even the most

skeptical historian has to postulate an "x," as M. Dibelius
put it, to account for the complete change in the behaviour
of the disciples, who at Jesus' arrest had fled and
scattered to their own homes, but who in a few weeks were
found boldly preaching their message to the very people
who had sought to crush the movement launched by Jesus by
disposing of its leader."[6] Fuller and other exegetes
do not hesitate to talk of the resurrection in terms of
revelation, the revelation, presumably, of Jesus' true
status vis-à-vis God. And the presupposition that the
New Testament is written "backwards" from this "revelatory
event" is as common, and needs as little documentation,
as any of the other kindred presuppositions already
mentioned. It means, I suppose, that the whole New Testament depicts Jesus in the status of Lord, Son of God,
Christ--a status of his which was first revealed "at" or
"after" the resurrection.

I, and many others I'm sure, have often recorded
our surprise, not to say dismay, at finding when we follow
the exegetes in search of this "event" which will show us
the first revelation of the true status of Jesus and thus
provide the historical source of our distinctive Christian faith, that we finally arrive at an uncertain and
highly inconclusive empty tomb, on the one hand, and,
on the other, at some "non-hallucinatory visions" enjoyed
by an uncertain number of individuals about which no
reliable details can be given. At this stage the first
revelation of the true status of Jesus seems remarkably
devoid of content. (What exactly was revealed? How
exactly was it revealed? Were words spoken? Deeds per-
formed by the risen One? What?) The light which was to
illumine His earthly life looks much like darkness, and the
faith which was here to find its source seems much more

needed for the "event" which was supposed to support it than it could possibly find any support in this "event."

But these points have already been made. And they have largely gone unheeded by the New Testament scholars. They have also largely gone unheeded by the systematicians[8] and for this there is less excuse, since attention to logical consistency is a professional requirement of the systematician in a way in which it is not required of the exegete. Normally, when such obvious logical problems are consistently either glossed over or ignored, we are likely to be in the presence of some very broad-rooted presuppositions indeed and it is time that we seriously investigated some of them.

Suppose for a moment that critical history were allowed to proceed with its search for the substantially recoverable historical data presented by the New Testament. We do after all say, that the distinctive Judaeo-Christian way of telling about God is to weave a story, a history, and not a theory; to tell the story while simultaneously conveying its significance for our ultimate concern. So it must be legitimate to ask: What can the critical historian recover from these texts, upon which the authors placed such significance? Surely the first substantial event which the critical historian will come upon is not the Resurrection of Jesus--at least if that is understood as an "event" in Jesus' own personal destiny in some sequence with birth, baptism and death.[9] The resurrection always seems to fade from us into the twilight zone of an uncertain sequence of visions. The first substantial event which critical history meets in its backwards probe is the *death* of Jesus.

The death of Jesus--a scandalous fact if ever there was one. Condemned, he died the common, cruel death of a

criminal. Some authors of the New Testament are already
trying to contain the full scandal of the cross, it seems.
For their own purposes they present Pilate as an unwilling
accomplice of "perfidious Jews." Thereby the radical
challenge of Jesus to all human lordship, a challenge
issued in behalf of the life-style of slaves, is muted.
But I do not believe that the New Testament authors as
a group went as far toward removing that scandal as their
later interpreters have gone. For us the death of this
man was not sufficiently revelatory of God's ways with
the world, it was not sufficiently inspirational or
salvific, and it was quite impotent to arouse faith.

Ignoring as best we could John's "he who sees me,
sees the Father," since the words were placed on the lips
of the merely earthly Jesus, ignoring above all John's
masterful *ecce homo* where the flesh in which God's word
is tabernacled is indicated in the person of a poor tat-
tered remnant of humanity; we wanted another "event"
because we wanted that first one reversed! That really
is the reaction of the truly scandalized.

We wanted a real revelation of a glorified Jesus so
that we could reasonably be expected to believe that he
was indeed the Son of God (we could not, of course, say
this with the centurion on Calvary). We wanted a resurrection after the death, and an ascension, an exaltation,
a session at the right hand, and we wanted witnesses to as
much of this as possible. We certainly needed witnesses
to his breathing of the Spirit on his followers since
(we could not seriously agree with John that his crucifixion
was his glory, his exaltation, his spirit-breathing). We
wanted another source for our faith besides Calvary so
that we could call him Son We could hardly be expected
to accept that "as Son, he learned faith through what he

suffered" (Heb 5:8), and in this same way, taught that
faith to us and made us sons. We wanted another
"event" and, since we are nothing if not resourceful, we
got one.

The history of recent exegetical scholarship has
been for us an unbroken sequence of frustration, whittling
away relentlessly at our revelation-event *par excellence*
and the historical source of our Christian faith. But
resourceful to the last, however minute the remaining
"event" left to us by the critical scholars, we have still
managed to make it do all that we demand of it. Dibelius's
"x" is still there, whatever it was, and whatever it was,
it founded the full Christian faith in Jesus, a faith
which previously was either impossible or just non-
existent, or had died with Jesus on the cross (a multiple
choice is provided at this point). Above all, the "x"
excused us from going back to the place where we did not
want to go, to the definitive revelation of God on Calvary.

I do not, of course, wish to maintain that none of
the first followers of Jesus or of the New Testament
writers thought of the resurrection of Jesus as a historically verifiable event of Jesus' own personal history
and, as such, a revelatory event additional to the other
events of his life and death. I do not have the exegetical
expertise to decide that issue and I learned long ago
from Unamuno that even an evangelist may sometimes unwit-
tingly allow the real truth to come through, rather than
tell it.[10] But especially Jewish Christians must have
been even more aware than are modern exegetes of the
fact that the early resurrection preaching is to a great
extent woven from Old Testament texts for the cultic
coronation ceremony of a Davidic king, and that much of
it must therefore have had the primary purpose of proposing

that the crucified one was Messiah, rather than of describing another event after Calvary.

Comparing the LXX texts of 2 Sam 7, Pss 2, 110, and 89, we note the following:

1. The king is declared God's son through Divine birth and/or adoption: "You are my son, today I have given birth to you" (Ps 2:7; cf. Pss 89:26-27; 110:3; 2 Sam 7:14). 2. The king is referred to as "Lord" *Kyrios* (Ps 110:1) or "the anointed one" *Christos* (Pss 2:3; 89:21, 39, 52) or "the elected one" (Ps 89:4, 19). 3. Reference is made to the greatness of his name (2 Sam 7:9), and if G. Von Rad is correct in identifying Isa 9:5-6 with this ritual,[11] "Wonderful Counselor, Mighty God, Everlasting Father, Prince of Peace" are throne names. 4. His kingship is proclaimed as representative and regent of God the King (Pss 2:6; 89:4, 18, 27, 29, 36; 2 Sam 7:12-13, 16, 17), and his sovereignty and judgment is announced over the forces of heaven and earth together with their subjection and subordination to his rule (Pss 2:809; 80:19-29). This Sovereignty is correlative to the supreme sovereignty of the Creator-King YHWH (Pss 89:5-14; 8). 5. He is said to be "exalted" (Pss 2:8; 89:14, 17-19, 25, 28; 110:1). In 2 Sam 7:12, this act of exaltation might well be implied in YHWH's promise: "I will raise up (anestēsō) your son (LXX "seed") after you." If so, it would be another and specific reason for the early church's use of these texts to describe the resurrection and exaltation of God's son, Jesus. 6. In connection with this fifth accent is a reference to the perpetuation of the king's lineage, the house of David (Pss 89:3, 4, 29, 34,-37; 2 Sam 7:12,

16, 25, 29). One should note the related term
"planting" in 2 Sam 7:10 and the disappointment
expressed over YHWH's apparent failure to keep his
promise (Ps 89:38-52). 7. Obedience and subordination to the will of God is expected of the king as
God's slave or servant *doulos* (cf. Pss 2:8; 89:4,
20, 30-32, 39, 50; 2 Sam 7:8, 14, 20, 25, 27, 29). 8.
The king as son is also an heir with an inheritance
(Ps 2:8). Finally, a unique idea should be mentioned,
since it receives such attention in the Epistle to
the Hebrews: the declaration in Ps 110:4 that the
king is "a priest forever according to the order of
Melchizedek."[12]

I have presented these accents simply as a reminder
to all that so much of the language of the earliest
resurrection preaching is not language suggested by a
new event, but rather language borrowed from a very old
institution, and that should give us the hint that the
primary purpose of this preaching is to persuade us that
the one we crucified, the *crucified one*, is God's anointed.

I do not wish in this context to develop an argument
concerning what I think the main thrusts of the New Testament texts on the resurrection to be. But I wish once
again to express grave doubts that the resurrection kerygma
of the New Testament can play the role we have all expected
it to play, namely, of providing us with some well-witnessed
event which could show us how the full Jesus-faith originated in history and which could in this way help justify
that faith. More than that, I would like to make a suggestion that I will try to carry through the rest of this
essay: we are forever looking for some well-documented
divine interventions, some unquestionably divine words or
acts, some clear signs from the heavens from which we can

derive the substance of our faith and its motivation. We
do not wish to find the substance of our faith in the
ordinary, the insignificant, the unpalatable, the weakness
of this world which was to confound its strength. We do
not wish to find faith's motivation in the spirit of a
man who tried to convey to all people and especially to
outcasts and sinners, in his words, his prayer, his ritual meals and above all in his service to them, that they
were the cherished children of God. So when we find in
the New Testament an unpalatable event together with a
statement of the true significance of the one who underwent it, we try as best we can to divide it into two dimensions if not two events, so that one part of the now
double event will be all too human but the other will be
clearly of divine origin. This is what we do with the
event we sometimes call death-resurrection. We thus
impose our own system, in particular our own understanding of revelation, on the source of Christianity and then,
most tragically of all, we mistake the true nature of
the faith of Jesus.

The Baptism

The baptism of Jesus was not, of course, nearly as
scandalous for his would-be followers as was his death.
But it must have been scandalous nonetheless. It seems
as if the movement begun by John the Baptizer was strong
and widespread in the years that saw the birth of Christianity (Acts 19:1-7), and of course, to followers of
John a man baptized by John would not automatically
qualify for any office, except perhaps that of disciple
of John (see the question posed by John's disciples in

Luke 7:18-25).

The baptism of John was, as the synoptics agree, a
baptism of repentance for the forgiveness of sins, a
ritual of conversion which prepared one for the coming
of God's reign. So those who came to John, the same
accounts tell us, were baptized in the Jordan, confessing
their sins. It was a cleansing, purifying, preparational
ritual (Matt 3:2, 6, 16; Luke 3:3, Mark 1:4-5). And Jesus,
his followers can neither forget nor deny, underwent it.
So perhaps the disciples of John were correct after all in
considering the Jesus movement questionable, at least
insofar as it tried to be distinct. Jesus pursued the
reign of God as a convert of John the Baptizer. He was
not even original insofar as he needed conversion before
he could convert. Indeed, perhaps he appeared as something of an upstart.

In the New Testament the accounts of the baptism of
Jesus and the references to it are now well-recognized
mixtures of polemics, christology and, of course, a rather
uncomfortable historical memory. The polemical interest
is satisfied by having John renounce titles, some of
which at least were applied to Jesus (this happens mainly
in John 1:19-24), by making John protest at Jesus being
baptized by him, and by putting on the lips of John words
of personal subordination and recognition of the one who
really had God's spirit and who really was God's son. The
christological interest, already obvious in the last point,
is clarified in the descent of the Spirit and the heavenly
word of the baptismal scene itself.

Probably because the baptism of Jesus is not quite
so scandalous as his death, the historical investigation
of this incident in his life does not get quite so much
attention and may not meet with quite the same resistance.

In the patrisic period, and indeed in most uncritical
views of the matter, the description of the baptism of
Jesus in the synoptics is taken to be factual throughout.
It is therefore the source and paradigm of Christian baptism. Thus the impression of a certain similarity with
the death/resurrection is unavoidable. Just as resurrection is deemed to be the historical source of Christian
faith itself, so the special divine "extras" in John's
baptism of Jesus--mainly the descent of the Spirit--pro-
vide the historical source for specifically Christian baptism, the initial ritual experience of the Christian
faith.

But it is just these similarities which sould alert
the critical historian. Is there, in addition to Jesus'
rather embarrassing baptism at the hands of John, some
special divine intervention of a revelatory nature which
took place on this occasion and which would remove the
scandal for those would-be followers of Jesus who either
witnessed or heard of this act of public repentance? The
coming of the Spirit, it is hardly necessary to remark,
is not a public revelatory event--one can hardly take
the dove literally. The presence of the Spirit is palpable, if at all, in the quality of a life, in the deeds
that are done, in the trials undergone and overcome.
Nothing that was visible at the moment of Jesus' baptism
in the Jordan could have told the participants that the
Spirit was descending in an unprecedented way. But what
of the voice from heaven? It is here that the similarity
with the resurrection kerygma is most striking. God is
made to declare that Jesus is his beloved son. Luke, in
fact, has "you are my beloved son" (not "this is my
beloved son") and some ancient manuscripts of Luke have,
instead of the usual following words "with thee I am well

pleased," the words "this day I have begotten you" (see
the R.S.V. note to Luke 3:22). Now this is the very
theme of the earliest resurrection kerygma we know:
Rom 1:4 talks of the resurrection in terms of Jesus being
designated Son of God. Luke himself in Acts 13:33 has
Paul's resurrection kerygma use that very quotation from
the old enthronement psalm (2:7): "you are my son, today
I have begotten you."

One can scarcely avoid the impression that we are
here in the presence of a kergymatic construction similar
to that which Jesus' followers produced after his death.
The primary theme of the old Davidic enthronement texts
is being used once again to say that the one we meet now
in the baptism is indeed God's son. Once again, if the
historian does his job well enough, he will not come upon
two events or even a double event, one event or part of
the event scandalous but the other of such a divinely
revelational character that it reverses the implications
of the first and successfully removes its scandal. Indeed,
if there were two events, our conclusion would have to
be that Jesus was son of God *in spite of* the fact that
John baptized him, i.e., in spite of what history left
to itself could tell us. But in fact the historian will
find just one event, Jesus' baptism by John the Baptizer,
and he knows already what that baptism meant. He will
then be told in the same context, by use of the old
enthronement theme and by reference to the coming of the
Spirit of God, that the one who is here baptized is son
of God.

There is no "in spite of" implied here. We are told
quite plainly that the one who cleanses and purifies himself in preparation for the coming of God's reign is
God's son, just as in the resurrection kerygma we are told

that the one who was judged a threat to the secure power
of both ecclesiastical and civic leaders and was executed
on such a charge, is God's son. Apparently in both cases,
the sonship is because of, not in spite of, what happened.
We may prefer a different kind of son of God. We normally
do. We may be secretly quite disappointed with the one
we got. We usually are. But that does not change the
reality of God's revelation.

On the other hand, we should resist the temptation
to think that because our New Testament writers are using
the theme "you are my son, this day I have begotten you"
for both baptism and resurrection, we are entitled to
conclude that they think and are telling us that on the
days of Jesus' baptism and his death, they could not
later think, without explicit revision, that he was made
son of God earlier at his baptism. But we have no evidence whatever for such revision. And, in the second
place, the whole hypothesis is quite unwarranted. The
preachers and writers were clearly borrowing a messianic
theme from the enthronement ceremony of the ancient
Davidic kings, and they are applying that theme to what
is clearly an entirely different type of situation. It
is obvious, then, that they feel the theme applies
because they believe Jesus fulfills all their messianic
hopes, though in a very unexpected way, not because the
details of the enthronement ceremony (for instance, that
the king was actually declared son only when he actually
became king) are applicable in any literal way. In no
way, then should we try to evade the point which is made
in the New Testament about baptism and death, namely,
that the one who was baptized by John and died as a criminal is God's son, and for these reasons rather than in
spite of them. If we insist that these early Christians
thought that they were describing, in addition to the

scandalous events of death and baptism specific divine
interventions which were either constitutive of Jesus'
sonship or literally revelatory of it, we are carrying
our own presuppositions to their texts and coming away
from the texts with our presuppositions still intact.

The Birth

We never really give up, though. We may not be
able to find in our normative scriptures any well-evidenced revelatory event accompanying baptism or death
which would take away the scandal. But we will discover
an extraordinary birth! We will have our son of God with
his divine credentials intact in historical records,
however difficult it may and however ingenious we may
have to be to find them.

The infancy gospels appear only in Matthew and Luke.
They have not drawn to themselves nearly as much real
scholarly attention as they deserve.[13] They are the
source of convictions concerning Mary and Jesus about
which many Christians, and particularly Roman Catholics,
prove to be very touchy. I shall therefore confine my
attention, in dealing with them, to the basic question
of this essay: What do they tell the critical historian?
And what do they then say to Christian faith? Above all,
what presuppositions can the systematician detect in some
of the usual ways of dealing with these infancy gospels?

It has long been recognized that the infancy gospels
are first and foremost christologies. That is to say,
their primary purpose is to express the messianic significance for us of the one whose conception, birth, infancy
(and, in Luke's case, youth) they narrate. Hence they
are woven, as are the passion narratives, from Old

Testament themes, most notably from narratives about
Abraham and Moses. As in the case of the resurrection
kerygma and the baptism pericopes, the theme of the coming
Spirit of God and the theme of the enthroned son of God
both appear with the obvious purpose of again conveying
the significance for our relationship with God of this
Jesus who was crucified, whom John baptized, and who was
born of a Jewish woman called Miriam. "The Holy Spirit
will come upon you, and the power of the Most High will
overshadow you; therefore the child to be born will be
called holy, the Son of God" (Luke 1:35). Matthew simply
has "that which is conceived in her is of the Holy Spirit"
(1:20), but later in the scene of the return from Egypt
the "son" theme appears in a quotation he uses: "Out of
Egypt have I called my son" (2:15).

The infancy gospels also contain their quota of
polemics as did the narratives of Jesus' baptism at the
hands of John. The polemical strain is perhaps most
obvious in Matthew, as one might expect if one remembered
Matthew's resurrection kerygma with its own heavy polemic
against Jewish stories about a stolen corpse (Matt 27:62-
28:15). Matthew clearly does not intend to let his
Jewish opponents get away with very much! It is almost
as difficult to decide what actual memories, if any,
underly the present infancy gospels, as it is to discover
by what means of transmission these could have reached
such relatively late documents as Matthew and Luke. But
the most likely content of such a memory, if there was
one, is that Jesus was conceived between the time that
Mary was betrothed (married) to Joseph and the time at
which he took her to his house, the latter being the time
at which legitimate marital relations could have taken
place. There is certainly evidence of early Jewish polemic

to the effect that Jesus was illegitimate--the "natural"
conclusion one would come to if the sequence of events
mentioned above had actually been remembered in any widespread way. Hence the need for a Christian polemic in
response.

Perhaps the most intriguing part of Matthew's counter-
polemic is found in the genealogy of Jesus, the son of
David, the son of Abraham, with which he opens his gospel.
He includes in his gospel genealogy the names of women,
as Luke does not; four women in fact, and what a selection
of women! Judah begot Perez by Tamar, his daughter-in-law,
who disguised herself as a prostitute in order to become
pregnant by him (Matt 1:3; cf. Gen 38:12-30). Salmon, next,
was the father of Boaz by Rahab, and the only Rahab we
know from the Old Testament is the famous prostitute of
Jericho (Matt 1:5; cf. Jos 2, 6). We know that Rahab was
"rehabilitated" in the course of the Rabbinic traditions
of the intertestamental period (cf. Megilloth 14b, 15a), at
least to the extent that her chosen profession was no
longer mentioned! She then appeared as ancestress of
prophets, of Huldah the instigator of the reform of Josiah
(2 Kings 22), and even of Jeremiah. She appears on two
other occasions in the New Testament: in Heb 11:31 as one
of the heroines of faith, and in James 2:25 as an example
of salvation by works. Thus, whether you are Protestant
or Roman Catholic, justified by faith or works, this
versatile lady will serve your interests! The point,
though, is not so much what she became in the course of
later traditions, but to notice just what kind of person
could and did become such a paragon of virtue. Boaz begot
Obed (for Naomi) of a Moabitess called Ruth as an act of
pure gratuity, for he was not even the nearest of kin
and she, as a foreigner, had no rights to him or to his

lineage (Matt 1:5; cf. the Book of Ruth). David, finally, begot Solomon of the wife of Uriah, in an adulterous act which David, when he failed to disguise his own paternity, further aggravated by the murder of Uriah (Matt 1:6; cf. 2 Sam 11).

Why, one wonders, are we reminded of this winsome foursome in the course of Jesus' genealogy--one who played the prostitute, one professional prostitute, one foreigner who bowed her way into favor and royal lineage, and one adultress? Why are we faced with an opening and closing reminder of adulterous conception, with one irregular marriage situation and the ubiquitous Rahab thrown in for good measure? Obviously the intent is to say that God does not necessarily elect those of unimpeachable pedigree to do his work in this world. For those who know their Jewish history, it was a powerful piece of pole- mic indeed. But what does it say to us? In the case of those who circulated a story that his followers stole Jesus' body Matthew could simply circulate another story to the effect that these people were lying in their teeth and that it paid them well to do so, and in this conten- tion he was undoubtedly correct. But apparently he could not as easily say that those who called Jesus illegitimate were lying, and so his polemic here has to be much more complex.

A second part of Matthew's polemic has Joseph per- form the naming ceremony for the child, thus legally mak- ing him his son, and giving him his Davidic lineage (Matt 1:25). But it is a third part of the polemic which most interests us at the moment: the part at which it joins the themes of Spirit and Son, themes in which we have already seen christology expressed at the moments of baptism and death. Here in the infancy gospels, by means

of the twin themes, polemics and christology are inter-
woven in a very complex way. Spirit is one of the most
ancient symbols in these Near Eastern cultures for God
and particularly for God's active presence in our world.
Son is one of the most powerful natural symbols known by
which to express the extension of one's favor to a person
who is the very continuation of one's effective presence
in the world. Naturally, then, as one can quite easily
see both from the description of Jesus' baptism and from
the resurrection kerygma, the primary result of saying
that the Spirit comes upon or is with or (even more so) is
breathed by Jesus, as of saying that Jesus is God's son,
is to convey the conviction that God acts in Jesus. But
the infancy gospels, once they go beyond the first two
forms of polemic outlined above, apparently intend also
to convey that the coming of the Spirit at Jesus' conception makes that a virginal conception and makes the conceived God's son. At least that seems to be the literal
impact of the Lukan text already quoted above (Luke 1:35).
It is precisely at this point where the themes of Spirit
and Son are used in a dual role, to describe Jesus' conception in addition to God's relationship to him, that we
have difficulty in understanding what exactly is being
conveyed. To be more precise: though we can well understand the meaning of the Spirit and Son themes in presenting God's relationship to Jesus, we have great difficulty in understanding these themes' bearing upon the
conception of Jesus. But why?

We do not wish to think of the Holy Spirit acting as
the male principle in the conception of Jesus. That would
make the birth of Jesus too much like that of some semi-
divine beings who were conceived, in other mythologies,
by the mating of a god with a human female. But then we

ask ourselves: Just what do we understand by the role of
the Spirit in the conception of Jesus and of Jesus' subsequent divine sonship? I do not really know the answer
to this question. I do not know what Luke in particular
had in mind. I can only hazard a guess that the Spirit
of God, if it did not act as the male principle and yet
Jesus was born from the body of Mary in an otherwise
natural way, must have supplied what was necessary to the
embryonic Jesus by an act such as creation out of nothing.
Jesus' being God's son *as a result of this act* (see Luke's
"therefore") could then mean only what Luke meant when
he calls Adam "the son of God" in his genealogy of Jesus
(Luke 3:38). To call Adam God's son there presumably
refers to the belief that Adam was created by God (out
of nothing, or out of "dust") and not derived in the normal way from parents. This explanation would mean that
the title Son of God had as little in common with its
meaning in the other christological moments, where it
refers to God's salvific activity in Jesus, as the coming
of the Spirit for conception has in common with the coming
of the Spirit at other christological moments. We should
simply find ourselves in the presence of two well-under-
stood symbols now put to a unique usage. And to what
purpose? Apparently to inform us that Jesus was conceived of one who nonetheless remained a virgin.

We are undoubtedly correct in seeing the infancy
gospels as, first and foremost, christologies, i.e.,
statements of the function and significance of Jesus as
he was known from his public life and even more public
death. Therefore we are undoubtedly correct also in concluding that the principal function of the themes of
Spirit and Son in the infancy gospels is identical with
the function of those same themes when they are used in

the rest of the New Testament: namely, the christological function, the functional description of Jesus as the one in whom God acted in the world. The function of these same themes in explaining the mode of Jesus' conception must then be a subsidiary one, and I think we must confess that it introduces as much obscurity to our inquiring minds as it throws light on the subject. For if we ask such questions as how Mary knew that the Holy Spirit somehow formed the embryonic Jesus in her womb, we either have her guessing this from the enormous improbability of a "natural" virginal conception, or we have her informed of this by a literal revelation from God (since creative acts of God are not naturally detectable). Then if we ask how Matthew and Luke knew of this action of the Holy Spirit, we have to suppose, in the absence of any real evidence, a tradition which was carried from Mary herself right down to the very different formulations of it in Matthew and Luke. (Matthew has the virginal conception announced to Joseph only) and Luke has it announced only to Mary. In the end, I think it safe to say, we have to believe on the word of these two evangelists, if that is our decision, that the Holy Spirit somehow formed the embryonic Jesus in his mother's womb; or we may believe this because the church to which we belong makes this part of its authoritative teaching.

But if we act, as we are also entitled to do, as critical historians, what shall we find we can say about the birth of Jesus? That it was obscure, to a point of unusual vulnerability. Obscure? Yes, absolutely unimpressively obscure. It is hard to say where he was born. Matthew gives the impression that his folks were native to Bethlehem, but had to move to Nazareth out of fear of Herod's son when they came back from Egypt. Luke, who has not heard that they were in Egypt, regards them as a Nazareth family who had to go to Bethlehem just when Jesus was born for a census which Matthew has not heard of. His native town is uncertain, and his parents are people of no significance whatsoever. The genealogies are obviously late and discordant attempts to give them royal lineage. And vulnerable? The very circumstances of his conception are clouded in suspicion which no naturally available evidence can disperse. Just imagine trying to tell someone that your son, whom they know to have been born seven months after your wedding and whom they consider with good cause to be a threat to both civil and ecclesiastical law and order, was conceived of the Holy Spirit. No wonder Matthew's triple polemic tries to cover all the bases. And this is God's son, in whom God's Holy Spirit comes, and on whom he remains? Yes.

The pattern holds. A man of obscure and, from the natural point of view, questionable birth, a man baptized by John the Baptizer's baptism of repentance for the forgiveness of sins, a man executed as a threat to ecclesiastical and civil law and order, this is God's son? Yes. And because of all this, not in spite of it. For there are no well-evidenced events of a divinely revelational character to remove the offense of birth, baptism and death. The scandal for the Jews and the folly for us Gentiles always remains intact in spite of all our misguided, half-theological half-historical attempts to get rid of the scandal and to have our Son of God and God's Spirit not in weakness but in strength, on our terms rather than his.

Conclusion

I have been trying to hint at something here which will take a much longer study to argue in detail. I offer it as a systematician's contribution to the contemporary quest of the historical Jesus. Whether the guest be termed new or old, it is and must be perennial for Christians who naturally consider the Founder normative for the faith of his would-be followers. There is a deep and contagious presupposition in our midst which concerns the very nature of the Christian faith. It is a vision of the essence of Christianity which affects equally the study of the sources and the perception of the person of the Founder. Though the vision unconsciously influences systematicians, exegetes and historical scholars alike, since the primary professional business of the systematician is to review critically the key vision or ideas which form the dynamic logic of any system of Christian myth or thought, it is also the proper responsibility of the systematician clearly and distinctly to identify this basic vision or idea, to deploy its logic for critical analysis, and to ask the critical questions about its own validity or adequacy. The manner in which a systematician goes about this task is difficult to explain, since there is no such thing as a method in systematic theology. Despite what most of the riders on the present methodological bandwagon would wish to convey, each system simply has its own "method," i.e., its own intrinsic logic. But normally, the basic, presupposed idea or view out of which a system is constructed comes into sight when that system is compared critically with others. Sometimes (and this is the case in the present essay), certain undue stresses in the logic of a system reveal at one and the same time the vision or idea out of which it is constructed and the resistance of some of the material used in the construction. This second approach to the center of a system can be particularly instructive when the material out of which it is constructed, as should normally be the case with Christian systems, is historical material concerning the Founder himself.

Most of us have been led to presuppose that the origin and indeed much of the substance of Christian faith lies in one or more acts of divine revelation adequately witnessed and indisputably emerging as acts of God, events on the historical record so far above anything our poor world is capable of that their divine source and their divine intent could not for one moment be mistaken by people of even minimal goodwill. The fact that our contemporary theology of revelation, when it did finally settle for a theory of divine revelation in the form of historical events, immediately fell foul of all the doubts and difficulties for which modern historical scholarship is renowned,[14] did not remove our presupposition about the incidence and nature of divine revelation, nor even seriously damage it. Dibelius's "x," together with other smaller "x's" like the baptism and birth, stood their ground in the unconscious depths of our theological minds from which our presupposed ideas wield their indomitable influence.

Somewhere at the back of our conscious minds we knew (or, if we did not, the historical scholars could quickly remind us), that his death was scandalous, his baptism odd, and the respectability of his human origins not easy to prove to the skeptical. But, then, our faith had its source and substance in incidents of indisputable divine

origin which accompanied these events, and not in the
events themselves. Our presuppositions not only remained
intact, they muscled the New Testament material unwill-
ingly into a supportive role. That the source of our faith
could be in a man whose birth was obscure and therefore
vulnerable to suspicion, whose baptism advertised him as
a convert, and who died the death of a condemned criminal;
that the substance of our faith should consist in the
deep conviction that obscure and despised illegitimates,
sinners and convicted criminals can say *Abba* to God, and
that the prostitutes can enter into God's kingdom before
the religiously respectable--that is not a vision which
we find easily compatible with the vision of our faith
which we normally presuppose. But it is one we should
soon consider, or reconsider.

The substance of this distinctive faith which Jesus
inspired in his followers, and of which he is therefore
the source in our history, could not of course be gleaned
simply from an analysis of birth, baptism and death alone.
Only a careful study of his public ministry, and particularly
of his experiences and understanding of the reign of God
which it was his mission to introduce, could fully yield
the substance of that distinctive faith. In light of
this, the full significance of his death would appear as
the justification for the use of the Spirit and Son sym-
bolism in the resurrection kerygma and in connection with
his birth and baptism. It was because he inspired and
enabled others to experience themselves, no matter who
or what they were, as equally cherished children of the
one Father and above all to treat each other as such
across all destructive human barriers, that this Jesus,
born of Mary, baptized by John, and crucified under
Pontius Pilate, is God's very son to his followers, and

the very embodiment of the Spirit of God in human history.

I wish to make a few further remarks on the subject of Christian faith and critical history. Bultmann is correct in one sense. Faith, being personal decision, does not depend upon the historian's labor, and it depends as little on the systematician's. No amount of exegetical or systematic expertise will allow me to say *Abba*, the Lord's Prayer. I can catch the faith which this prayer both expresses and requests only by contagion from those who, no matter what I have been or now am, treat me too as a son of God. This alone will enable me, if anything ever will, to experience God as Father and to treat others in turn as his children.

But if Bultmann is correct in one way, Renan is just as surely wrong in another. Absolute faith is not necessarily incompatible with sincere history. In fact, where Christian faith is in question quite the contrary is the case. For where such faith is truly present, it should be able to recognize itself in the New Testament. And even where, as with so many of us, only a counterfeit version is present, good critical scholarship, the kind that can be produced by a combination of system and history, can at least expose the counterfeit for what it is and point to the real thing, though scholarship in itself is quite incapable of putting *that* in our possession.

Christian faith and critical history are natural allies, not natural enemies. The dichotomy which the critical period introduced between faith and history was due to a misunderstanding of one (faith) and a failure to press the other (history) to its fullest possibilities and its final results. The faith of Jesus, radical as it is, is not outside the human historian's range. A mixture of confusion and fear put it outside of our

intellectual grasp: confusion about the nature of faith
due to our preconceptions, and fear of pressing our investigations sufficiently far.   Perhaps we did not wish to
disturb religious authorities (as Jesus did in his time);
perhaps, more honest now, we were afraid of the awful
challenge of what we might find.   Glorious sons of God,
odd as it might seem, are much easier to manage then the
one who was finally sent, and glorious representatives of
glorious sons of God, resplendent in title and raiment,
are much easier to placate than those who truly serve and
thus lay upon us the claim that we should be servants in
turn.   But it is never too late for scholarship to get
its act together and to play its admittedly contributory
role.   And it is never too soon.   The world is still rid-
den by the quest for dominating power and envious glory,
in churches as well as states, and service to genuine human
needs is still available only at prohibitive prices.

Notes

[1]New York: Modern Library, 1955, p. 65.

[2]R. Bultmann, *The Theology of the New Testament*
I (New York: Scribner's, 1951), p. 26.

[3]G. W. F. Hegel, *Lectures on the Philosophy of
Religion* I (London: Routledge & Kegan Paul, 1895), pp.
28-29.

[4]The point was elaborated in a paper entitled
"Philosophical Hermeneutics and Theological Hermeneutics"
presented by Paul Ricoeur to the Berkeley Center for
Hermeneutical Studies, November 1975.

[5]M. Kähler, *The So-called Historical Jesus and the
Historic, Biblical Christ* (Philadelphia: Fortress Press,
1964), p. 56.

[6]*The Formation of the Resurrection Narratives* (New
York: Macmillan, 1972), p. 2.

[7]I read that phrase somewhere in a recent christology.
I forget the context, but I remember the phrase as one
of the finest question-begging phrases to be found even
in a theology text.

[8]As I noted in a review of the latest christologies,
of Küng and Kasper, in *The Living Light* 14 (1977), pp. 147-
54.

[9]I mean to argue at length elsewhere that the New
Testament, in preaching the resurrection of Jesus, is
primarily interested in affirming his presence as Spirit
palpable in the Christian community, and not primarily in
his appearances to particular individuals as proof of a

personal event of his own survival.

[10]Miguel de Unamuno, *Our Lord Don Quixote* (Princeton: University Press, 1976), p. 105.

[11]Gerhard von Rad, "Das jüdaische Königsritual," *Theologische Literaturzeitung* 72 (1947), pp. 211-76.

[12]Insights are taken from an as yet unpublished paper by my colleague John H. Elliott of the University of San Francisco.

[13]Though that situation is likely to be improved now with the appearance of Raymond Brown's *The Birth of the Messiah* (New York: Doubleday, 1977).

[14]For more detail on theories of revelation and their relationship to the understanding of Christian faith see my *The Problems of Religious Faith* (Chicago: Herald Press, 1972).

THE RESURRECTION NARRATIVES IN RECENT STUDY

Reginald H. Fuller

When I wrote *The Formation of the Resurrection Narratives* in 1969-70 (published in 1971), it seemed that hardly anything had been written in English on the Easter narratives since A. M. Ramsey's *The Resurrection of Jesus Christ* (1946). For a full-length study of those narratives one had to go back to Kirsopp-Lake's, *The Historical Evidence for the Resurrection of Jesus Christ* (New York: Putnam, 1907), or at least to P. Gardner Smith, *The Narratives of the Resurrection* (London: Methuen, 1926). Since 1970, however, there has been a spate of books in English, French and German. Among those in English known to me would be:

-E. L. Bode, *The First Easter Morning* (Rome: Pontifical Biblical Institute, 1970) attempts to work back through the evangelists' redaction of the empty tomb stories and through the oral tradition to what really took place historically.

-W. Marxsen, *The Resurrection of Jesus of Nazareth* (London: SCM, 1970). This book is the English translation of *Die Auferstehung Jesu von Nazareth* (1968), a series of lectures for non-theological students given at the University of Münster. It is written from a thoroughly Bultmannian point of view.[1]

-C. F. D. Moule and D. Cupitt, "The Resurrection--A Disagreement," *Theology* 75 (1972), pp. 507-19. Cupitt

argues that Easter faith is a product of theological
reflection on the meaning of Jesus' history, and that
the Easter stories are merely projections of this
reflection. Moule argues more traditionally for a
transcendent cause for the resurrection faith.

-Raymond E. Brown, *The Virginal Conception and the
Bodily Resurrection of Jesus* (New York: Paulist,
1973) contains two essays, one his Union Theological
Seminary inaugural lecture and the other concerned
with the resurrection as protrayed in the New Testament narratives.

-Gerald O'Collins, *The Resurrection of Jesus Christ*
(Valley Forge: Judson, 1973). This book is divided
into three parts, the first dealing with the historical basis of the Easter faith, the second with that
faith itself, and the third with resurrection theology.
It takes issue with Bultmann and his followers.
O'Collins is a theologian rather than a biblical
scholar, and it is a pity that he spent so much time
on the biblical part about which he has little that
is original to say, rather than on the third part in
which he could have contributed much more.

-Peter Selby, *Look for the Living* (Philadelphia: Fortress, 1976), subtitled "The Corporate Nature of
Resurrection Faith." The main thrust of this book is
theological, discussing the issues with Pannenberg,
Moltmann, Marxsen, H. A. Williams, Künneth and others.
Some of his criticisms are very incisive from a biblical point of view, especially his criticism of those
who, like H. A. Williams,[2] treat the resurrection as
a symbol for the general experience of renewal.
Selby insists strongly on the christological, causa-
tive character of the event of Jesus' resurrection.

When, however, he comes to construct his own theology,
which includes a brief treatment of the Easter narratives, it is disappointing in its treatment of the
objective fact of Easter, and as the subtitle indicates deals mainly with its ecclesial effects.
   -Norman Perrin, *The Resurrection According to Matthew,
   Mark and Luke* (Philadelphia: Fortress, 1977), a
   redactional study of the Easter narratives in the
   synoptics. Characteristically, to the end Perrin
   refused to touch the Fourth Gospel, though there is
   really no justification for omitting it in a study of
   the history behind the resurrection faith, which he
   finds exclusively in 1 Cor 15:5-8.

   In this essay I would like first to note some points
of consensus, and then go on to discuss major points of
disagreement, taking issue principally with Marxsen and
some aspects of Perrin.

Meaning of the Resurrection Tradition

   There is remarkable unanimity that the tradition in
1 Cor 15:3 ff. forms the sole reliable basis for recon-
structing the history of the first Easter.
        (For I delivered to you as of first importance
            What I also received,
        that) Christ died for our sins
            in accordance with the scriptures,
        (that) he was buried,
        (that) he was raised the third day
            in accordance with the scriptures
        (and that) he appeared to Cephas,
        then to the Twelve.

Then he appeared to
> more than 500 brethren at one time,
> (most of whom are still alive
> though some have fallen asleep).

Then he appeared to James
then to all the apostles.
(last of all, as to the untimely born,
> he also appeared to me).

The parenthesized parts of the above quotation would
be generally recognized as Pauline additions. The non-
Pauline remainder is about as ancient as any tradition in
the New Testament could be. For Paul wrote 1 Cor about
55, and was referring to a tradition here which he had
delivered to the community when he formed it in 49-50.
But he says he had "received" these traditions. The very
latest moment when he received them would have been c. 35,
at his first post-conversion visit to Jerusalem (Gal 2:18-
20), since on that occasion he states that he say the two
people named in these traditions, viz. Cephas and James
the brother of the Lord. Some of the tradition may even
go back to Damascus in 33. There is one dissenting voice
here, and that is Marxsen. In a long and difficult argument he proposes that it was only Peter who had--or thought
he had--a vision of the resurrected Christ. Through whatever he experienced, Peter came to believe that Christ was
resurrected. It was through Peter's communication of his
experience to others that they, too, came to believe, and
then they in turn expressed their belief in Peter's language, asserting that they, too, had seen Jesus risen
(although what they actually meant was that they had come
to Easter faith). In Marxsen's words, "their faith, the
manifold functions they exercised, are all in the ultimate
resort based on the first appearance to Peter."[3] To

suppose this, Marxsen contends, eases certain historical problems. First, if this is the case, we need not suppose that Peter received more than one appearance, viz., that to himself. He was not included in the appearance to the Twelve and the one to all the apostles, not that to the 500, as the normal view necessitates. But we may ask, why should he not have had more than one appearance? Marxsen's difficulty is that such later appearances would no longer be constitutive for his other functions--as a member of the Twelve, as a member of the believing community, as a missionary (the appearance to all the apostles). But we may well agree with Marxsen on the decisive priority of the Lord's appearance to Peter. For it was this that led him to take the momentous step of summoning the scattered community of the Twelve and thus in a very literal sense, he was the rock on which the Church was built. Second, the reader will have noticed that Marxsen, as I have reported him, hedges on Peter's actually having seen Jesus. This is because he regards the language, "saw Jesus" as equivalent for having come to believe:

> After Good Friday, Simon was the first who arrived at faith in Jesus. But we must not phrase this historical conclusion as 'Simon was the first to see Jesus.' The relationship between believing and seeing must be expressed as follows: Simon was the first to believe; the reason for his having believed is expressed by saying that Simon saw Jesus.[4]

the trouble with this argumentation is that it confuses cause with effect. Peter's believing (as the parallel case of Paul demonstrates) is the *result* of his seeing, not the same thing. All biblical faith is response to encounter with revelation. I find it incredible that Marxsen indulges in such torturous arguments to prove otherwise. Incidentally, he follows this chapter with a

discussion of Paul's similar claim that he saw the risen
Lord. Here again Marxsen seems to confuse two different
entities, this time the resurrection itself and the post-
resurrection appearances. It is perfectly true, as Marxsen
says, that Paul was not "a witness of the resurrection."[5]
Neither Paul nor anyone else saw God raise Jesus from the
dead. But Paul never claimed that he did. Paul is quite
clear that it was because he saw the risen Lord on the road
to Damascus that he came to believe in the resurrection.
He never confused cause and effect in the way Marxsen does.
Christ's resurrection, the Damascus vision, and Paul's
coming to faith were distinguishable events, the second
after and because of the first.

This however is only a comparatively minor issue
raised by Marxsen. The great issue is what the resurrection itself actually is. According to Marxsen, a disciple
of Bultmann, it is a mythological way of saying *"Die Sache
Jesu geht weiter"*--everything that Jesus stood for, his
proclamation, his bringing God near to man in word and
deed, continues, despite the crucifixion. One might
say that, for Marxsen,

> The body of Jesus lies a-moulding in the grave
> But his cause goes marching on.

Once again, Marxsen is confusing cause with effect. It is
true that everything that Jesus stood for is being carried
on, that God in Christ draws near to us in judgment and
forgiveness in the kerygma of the church and in the faith
response of the community. But this happens and can only
happen precisely because God raised Jesus from the dead.
That is the witness of the earliest kerygma, and it under-
lies every page of the New Testament. The earliest kerygma (see the speeches of Peter in Acts 2 and 3, and the
Marcan passion predictions) proclaims the resurrection in

terms of man's No and God's Yes. Jesus' enemies nailed
him to the tree, but God raised him from the dead. The
resurrection is proclaimed in the New Testament as an act
of God. Of course it is true that this is never *narrated*
as an event--only the empty tomb and the appearances are
treated in that way. The resurrection is therefore in a
sense an inference from the actual experiences of the
disciples at Easter. But the faith to which the appearances led was the faith that God has resurrected Jesus
from the dead, and it was because of that, that the cause
of Jesus was able to continue.

Redactional Perspectives in Mark

I turn now to Norman Perrin's book. As we have
already noted, this book is a study of the redaction of
the Easter narratives in the synoptic gospels. Perrin
devoted the last years of his life to a redactional study
of Mark, and therefore it is in the chapter on Mark that
he is most original. For the other chapters, those on
Matthew and Luke, he relies mainly on the redactional
work of others, though there too he makes some interesting
contributions. Perrin's purpose represents a novel approach
to the Easter narratives. It seeks to define redactional
concerns which have been discovered in the pre-Easter
narratives and to apply these systematically as a clue to
the interpretation of the post-resurrection narratives.
Since Perrin's book has appeared quite recently, let
me first summarize what he has to tell us about Mark's
post-resurrectional narrative. He divides his analysis
into three parts: The Women at the Cross (Mark 15:40-41);
The Women at the Burial (15:42-27); and The Women at the
Empty Tomb (16:1-8). He argues, and I think most of us

would agree today, that Mark deliberately intended to end his gospel with *ephobounto gar* at 16:8. In other words, Mark never intended to narrate any appearance stories. The end has not been accidentally lost, nor was the gospel accidentally left unfinished. From this Perrin concludes that Mark's understanding of the resurrection is radically different from Paul who lists appearances, and from other evangelists who narrate them. Perrin seeks Mark's reason for this radical departure in three factors: 1) Mark's interpretation of the passion; 2) the meaning of Jesus' promise to go before his disciples into Galilee (14:28; 16:7); and 3) the roles of the women and the disciples in Mark's gospel.

Let us take each point in turn. First, Mark's interpretation of the passion. Here Perrin draws on his earlier work on the central section of Mark's gospel (8:26-10:45).[6] This central section is characterized by the passion predictions (8:31; 9:31; 10:33). Perrin notes how these predictions foretell the passion in a crescendo of detail but refer to the resurrection all three times in the same terse statement,"after three days he will rise again." From this Perrin concludes that Mark is interested in the resurrection not *per se*, but only as a prelude to something else. What that something else is, he concludes, is shown by the transfiguration story. He argues from the phrase "after six days" at the introduction of the transfiguration (cf. "after three days" in the resurrection prediction) and from the command to the three disciples to remain silent about it until after the resurrection, that Mark intends the transfiguration to be symbolic of the post-resurrection situation. Jesus after Easter is in heaven like Moses, awaiting his return in the parousia. Mark undergirds this parousia concern with the predictions in 9:1; Chapter 13 (the synoptic apocalypse); and 14:62.[7]

Second, as in his earlier work, Perrin takes the
references to "seeing" Jesus (*opsesthe, opsontai*) in 14:28
and 16:7 to refer not to the disciples seeing him in a
resurrection appearance, but to their seeing him at the
parousia.

Third, the role of the disciples and the women.
In Mark the disciples appear almost wholly in negative
terms. They misunderstand Jesus, first his parables and
miracles then especially his intention to go up to Jerusalem and face death. They cannot cast out demons at the
foot of the mountain of transfiguration; one of them
betrays him, the rest flee, and finally one of them denies
him. Thus they all disappear from the narrative. Then
the women take over the role one would have expected the
disciples to fulfill. Women anoint him before the passion
and after burial, they stand at the foot of the cross.
They discover the empty tomb and the fact of the resurrection. But then they too fail, for they do not convey the
message of the angel to the disciples. For Mark, both
the disciples and the women symbolize the "possibilities
and actualities of discipleship in the Christian communities which Mark knows and for which he writes."[8] So 14:28
points not to the disciples' restitution through a resurrection appearance but to the judgment of the imminent parousia.

What are we to make of this? Its brilliance no one
can deny. But perhaps it is just here that its danger
lies. At the recent San Antonio Colloquy on the gospels,
a classical scholar warned New Testament scholars that in
both fields the rarity of discovery of new materials for
us to work on leads to our constantly having to come up
with new theories about old materials. You can always
be original by calling into question something nobody else

has questioned before! That of course does not refute new
theories. But it does recommend caution. In any case, I
have difficulties about Perrin's interpretation. Everything really hangs on Mark 9:9; 14:28 and 16:7. But Mark
9:9, by implication, looks forward to and indeed sanctions
the apostolic preaching after the resurrection. How could
the Twelve preach unless they first were rehabilitated?
This therefore requires that the verb *opsesthe* in 14:28
and 16:7 imply the disciples' rehabilitation and must
refer therefore not to the parousia, but to the resurrection appearances (in itself, *opsesthe* could refer to either).
Moreover, the location of this seeing in Galilee suggests
to me that Mark is thinking of the resurrection appearances
rather than of the parousia. That Galilee was especially
connected with the parousia was a suggestion of Ernst
Lohmeyer which has no foundation that I know of, but which
many have uncritically repeated since.[9] But we do know of
traditions of resurrection appearances in Galilee (Matt
28:16-20; John 21).

The reference to Peter also argues for an appearance
rather than for the parousia, for Peter had no special connection with the latter (cf. 1 Cor 15:5). I have never
been able to persuade myself that the words "they said
nothing to anyone for they were afraid" meant that the
women did not deliver the angel's message to the disciples.
For one thing, we probably have here an "aporia" created
by the insertion of the Marcan redactional verse (16:7)
into an earlier tradition (16:8). The silence of the
women at the earlier stage of the tradition registered
the experience of mysterious revelation. Mark could have
continued to understand it that way, without intending to
suggest that the women failed to deliver the message.

Why then did Mark fail to narrate resurrection

appearances? In my *Formation of the Resurrection Narratives* I suggested the reason that the narratives of such appearances had not yet developed in Mark's community.[10] Like Paul (1 Cor 15:5 ff.), all he knew of was a *list* of appearances. It is just such a list he is drawing on (to Peter, to the Twelve) in the wording of 16:7.

Interpreting the Empty Tomb

There is widespread and growing consensus in Germany, Britain and in this country, that the empty tomb is what Bultmann called a "late legend." This is the view of most recent books, except some Roman Catholic and some conservative evangelical ones. The one refreshing exception in the critical camp is the radical theologian but rather conservative New Testament scholar, John A. T. Robinson, who in his new book, *Can We Trust the New Testament?*,[11] expresses his confidence that the empty tomb is a historical fact. The case for its late origin and legendary character rests upon two factors. The first is the silence of Paul. Some have argued that the empty tomb is in fact implied by the reference to the burial in the pre-Pauline tradition in 1 Cor 15:4a. Others have argued that Paul's argumentation about the bodily character of the general resurrection later in the same chapter imply the empty tomb. Against this, one German scholar (E. Güttgemanns)[12] has gone so far as to claim that while Paul held to the bodily character of the general resurrection, he did not accept it for Jesus! But the Achilles' heel of that suggestion is Phil 3:21, "he shall change the body of our humiliation and make it like his glorious body." We shall have to admit the silence of Paul. But at the same time

nothing he says about the resurrection is necessarily inconsistent with the tradition of the empty tomb.

But the real argument in favor of the empty tomb is
that the story in Mark 16:1-9 is not an *ad hoc* compilation
of the Evangelist, but has a long history behind it.
Norman Perrin used to say that in dealing with the gospel
materials is it always necessary to write a history of
the tradition. He applied that very faithfully in his
Rediscovering the Teaching of Jesus,[13] but signally omitted
to do so in his recent discussion of the empty tomb pericope, confining himself instead to the evangelist's redactional use of it. In my book I tried to reconstruct the
tradition and in peeling away the successive layers I
believed I could recover an original nucleus, a report of
Mary Magdalene (and perhaps other women: their names vary
in the tradition while in John they are entirely absent),
to the effect that she had discovered the tomb empty. Now
this is in itself a highly ambiguous fact, which it is
interesting to compare with the circumstances of Jesus'
birth. In both the Matthean and Lucan infancy narratives
we have the potentially scandalous fact that Mary became
pregnant before marriage. This fact was susceptible to
at least two discreditable interpretations. Nevertheless,
Christian faith interpreted this as a pneumatic conception
in a virgin, and expressed its faith in the literary form
of an annunciation narrative, using an *angelus interpres*
to convey the faith interpretation. I believe something
of the kind has happened with the story of the discovery
of the empty tomb. As a pure fact this too could be
given--as it has been given in the course of history--
various natural explanations, some of them discreditable
to the parties concerned. But Christian faith gave it a
different interpretation, an interpretation based on a

faith engendered by the resurrection appearances not by
the discovery of the empty tomb itself, any more than it
was Jesus' dubious birth that actually gave rise to the
belief in his Messiahship. Christian faith, then expressed
itself by the similar device of an *angelus interpres* who
announces the true meaning of the fact as seen by faith:
"He is not here; God has raised him."

Now of course it cannot be proven that Mary Magdalene
actually discovered the empty tomb. All we can claim for
it is that it belongs to the earliest recoverable tradition. As such, however, it was taken into and formed an
integral part of the New Testament proclamation. At the
same time, however, the empty tomb taken by itself could
be dangerously misleading. For it could suggest that the
raising of Jesus was the raising of his earthly body as
it was before, in other words a resuscitation rather than
an eschatological transformation. But even Mark intends
to safeguard the fact of eschatological transformation
by his use of the words, "He is not here," in the angelic
proclamation, while the other gospels add appearance stories
which adequately safeguard the eschatological transformation. This is true even of the later more materialized
stories of Luke and John, in which the Resurrected One
exhibits his bodily character by inviting touch and by
eating in their presence. These elements doubtless spring
from apologetic motives. But even in these later stories
Christ appears and disappears in a different mode of
existence.

The Historicity of the Resurrection

Whether the resurrection is to be described as a

historical fact or not is an issue that continues to be
much discussed. On the one hand we have the Bultmannians,
who regard it as a mythological expression of something
else, the rise of Easter faith, or the continuation of
Jesus' cause. On the other hand we have not only the conservative critics like A. M. Ramsey who insist on its
historicity,[14] but also the more recent Pannenberg school
who insist that it is definitely an event in history,
though not open to historical investigation.[15] It is clear
to me that the resurrection is *not* definable as an historical event for the following reasons: 1) its occurrence
was not actually witnessed or at least no one claimed to
have witnessed it; 2) its occurrence is not actually
narrated in the New Testament; 3) it is attested only in
kerygmatic assertion.

But as I argued in the *Formation of the Resurrection
Narratives* there is also a very important *theological*
reason why the resurrection should not be categorized as
a historical event. Since, as members of the Pannenberg
school have themselves demonstrated, resurrection is by
definition an eschatological event, occurring at the *end*
of history, i.e., precisely at the point where history
stops, it cannot by definition be historical but must
occur at the point where history is transcended. This is
not however to be taken as a denial in the Bultmannian
sense that anything "happened." As one of Bultmann's
partners in the demythologizing controversy put it, something happened after Good Friday between God and Jesus, and
not just between God and the disciples. As I understand
the certainly mythological-apocalyptic language of resurrection, it asserts that God created a new eschatological
existence for Jesus of Nazareth, outside this present
age, and from that future age he communicated himself by

revelatory encounters in this age. The resurrection is *sui generis*, for up to this point (with the possible exception of the Virgin Mary and the blessed saints) no other resurrection has yet occurred.

Notes

---

[1] I will discuss some features of this work later in this essay.

[2] H. A. Williams, *Jesus and the Resurrection* (London: SCM, 1951).

[3] W. Marxsen, *The Resurrection of Jesus of Nazareth* (Philadelphia: Fortress, 1970), p. 92.

[4] Ibid., pp. 95-96.

[5] Ibid., p. 107.

[6] N. Perrin, "The Use of (Para) Didonai in Connection with the Passion of Jesus in the New Testament," *A Modern Pilgrimage in New Testament Christology* (Philadelphia: Fortress, 1974), pp. 94-103.

[7] N. Perrin, *The Resurrection According to Matthew, Mark and Luke* (Philadelphia: Fortress, 1977), pp. 24-25.

[8] Ibid., p. 30.

[9] E. Lohmeyer, *Galiläa und Jerusalem* (Göttingen, Vandenhoeck & Ruprecht, 1936).

[10] R. H. Fuller, *The Formation of the Resurrection Narratives* (New York: Macmillan, 1971), pp. 64-68.

[11] J. A. T. Robinson, *Can We Trust the New Testament?* (Grand Rapids: Eerdmans, 1977).

[12] E. Güttgemanns, "'Text' und 'Geschichte' als Grundkatagorien der Generativen Poetik. Thesen zur aktuellen Diskussion um die 'Wirklichkeit' der Auferstehungstexte," *Linguistica Biblica* 11/2 (1972), pp. 2-12.

[13] N. Perrin, *Rediscovering the Teaching of Jesus* (New

York: Harper & Row, 1967).

[14]A. M. Ramsey, *The Resurrection of Christ* (Philadelphia: Westminster, 1956).

[15]W. Pannenberg, *Jesus--God and Man* (Philadelphia: Westminster, 1968), pp. 66-73.

"HE APPEARED TO ME":

1 Cor 15:8 as Paul's Religious Experience of the "End Time"

Geffrey B. Kelly

Interpretations of the resurrection narratives in
the Christian scriptures often seem to veer to extremes.
At the far right of the exegetical center, fundamentalists
will accept nothing less than an affirmation of the literal
exactness and true-to-lifeness of the gospel and epistle
texts with little or no regard to literary form or the
author's precise theological intent. Interpreters of an
extreme liberal ilk would, on the other hand, dismiss as
irrelevant the imagery of apparition or empty tomb accounts
and would smugly rejoice should some enterprising archeolo-
gist ever dig out the Christ skeleton from some long hidden
burial plot in Palestine. Bodily resurrection for these
latter must somehow fit into a preconceived philosophical
pattern and the bodily resurrection of Jesus be reduced
solely to a faith-dominated inner awareness of the early
Christian believers. Without wishing a pox on the houses
of both extremes, it should be observed at the outset of
this essay that the truth about the resurrection appearances
probably lies in the middle terrain between insistence
on Jesus' bodily reanimation to a just-as-before tangi-
bility and the reduction of Jesus' appearances to purely
interior, spiritual experiences.[1]
       To avoid the grief of either extreme we rely for this
middle ground on Paul's own contention that Jesus' bodily

resurrection involved the most radical transformation of his earthly body, but a bodily transformation linked in definite continuity with the Jesus who was raised and whose appearances provoke the recognition which is foundational for Paul's acceptance of Christ and for his later preaching. In this essay we will analyze the biblical texts in which Paul claims to have "seen" this risen Jesus and, from these, draw conclusions on the nature of Paul's "vision," its implications for Pauline theology and for a deeper understanding of the meaning of Christ's resurrection to believers of any age.

Paul and the Early Resurrection Tradition

Paul's account of the post-resurrection appearances of Jesus in 1 Cor 15 is significant because it is not only the first scriptural mention of these appearances but his assertions are also rooted in the earliest tradition and in Paul's personal testimony of having "seen" the risen Jesus. Paul states explicitly in vs.3a that he proclaimed the salvific death, burial and resurrection of Jesus on the basis of the tradition he had himself received. "I delivered (*paredōka*) to you as of primary importance what I also received (*parelabon*)." While it is controverted whether or not the core words of the tradition Paul cites were Greek translations of an Aramaic original,[2] it is clear that the technical language antedates Paul's own conversion and hence belongs probably to the first decade of the Christian church.

What is not so clear is the precise point where Paul splices his personal experience and sources into the original tradition. Most exegetes would include at the

very least in this pre-Pauline material the vss. 3b to 5a
where mention that Christ "appeared to Cephas" (*ōphthē*
Kēpha) is backed up by the pre-Lukan kerygmatic formula,
"he appeared to Simon" (*ōphthē Simōni*) of Luke 24:34.[3]
Even though Paul's arrangement of the names and groups
which follow defies both chronological ordering or precise
geographical location of sources, his delineation of witnesses is so carefully balanced in alternating clauses
that some evidence of his own redactional technique and
personal purpose emerges.[4] What is more important for our
present consideration, however, is that the list culminates
in vs. 8 in Paul's contention that Christ appeared to him.
"Last of all, as to one born out of proper time, he also
appeared to me" (*eschaton de pantōn hōsperei tō ektrōmati*
ōphthē kamoi). This pivotal assertion leads naturally
into the main point of 1 Cor 15, Paul's explanation of the
theological significance of the resurrection for the general resurrection of the dead.

Paul's Vision of Jesus as Authentication of His Ministry

Because Paul is trying to synchronize a confessional
formula which features the resurrection of Jesus, diverse
claims about witnesses to Jesus' post-resurrection appearances, and the climactic experience of his own vision,
with theological conclusions about the bodily resurrection
hoped for by Christians, it is difficult to unravel his
precise purpose as the emphasis in each section of 1 Cor
15 shifts.[5] Was Paul merely using the early tradition to
prove the "reality" of Jesus' bodily resurrection? This
is the opinion defended by Karl Rengstorf who, in a lengthy
study of the primitive resurrection tradition, argues
that the repeated pre-Pauline phrase, "he appeared"

($\bar{o}phth\bar{e}$), springs from the polemical and apologetic preoccupation of the early community. The phrase, he contends,
is rooted in the classic Septuagintal language to refer
to God's making visible a hidden reality.[6] When opponents
of the primitive Christian community attempted to denigrate
the claims that Jesus had appeared by labeling them purely
"subjective experiences," the community's defense took the
form of a deliberate coopting of the Septuagintal language
with all its connotation of visibility. Rengstorf calls
this "the earliest protest of Christianity accessible to
us, while it was still on the soil of the primitive community in Palestine, a protest against the attempt to
divest the Easter event of its objective character and
thereby to turn it from God's cause into that of the disciples."[7] Even if we can detect some apologetic purpose
like this in Paul's citing of the traditional verses of
3b-5, it is still doubtful whether Rengstorf's protrayal
of the earliest resurrection tradition's "sole" purpose
can be sustained, given the fact that the primitive community did not gear its kerygma to "prove" the resurrection at all. Rather, the tradition simply *affirmed* the
resurrection and its eschatological significance by insisting that it occurred on the third day *in fulfillment of
the scriptures*.[8] The testimony of the scriptures thus
became the most telling evidence for the fact of the resurrection in the earliest apostolic preaching. Reginald
Fuller even suggests that Paul may have been the *first* to
begin to use the appearances as *evidence* of Jesus' resurrection.[9]

If such was Paul's purpose, the appearances would seem
at cursory glance to constitute imposing evidence indeed,
especially if Paul is appealing to living witnesses who
could be interrogated. This presupposes, of course, that

the verb "appeared" [to] or "was seen" [by], or equivalent translations of the Greek ōphthē, refers to physical sight of a being having some degree of corporeality.[10] As we will note below, this kind of vision cannot be aprioristically excluded.[11] Yet, it is more evident that Paul's primary purpose here is not so much to give a "seeing is believing" proof of Christ's resurrection as to authenticate his own ministry and, thereby, to confer authority on his preaching of the significance of Jesus' resurrection for the faith and hope of the Christian community. The appearance of the risen Jesus is for Paul intimately associated with his vocation to apostleship. Through this experience he was both brought to Christianity and inspired to carry forward the work of reconciliation begun in Jesus' lifetime.

Extrapolating from the context of 1 Cor 9 and 15, moreover, it is likely Paul found himself constrained to establish the authenticity of his mission and message by an appeal to credentials on a par with the other apostles who had walked with Jesus and had themselves seen Jesus alive after his resurrection.[12] This becomes more imperative in the light of Paul's previous persecution of Christians and of his need to associate his apostleship with a direct commission from the Lord rather than indirectly through a less imposing instruction and assignment from the Jerusalem community. Hence in his letter to the Galatians he insists that after the "revelation" he had received, he did *not* go up to Jerusalem to consult with the apostles but went immediately instead to Arabia and then returned to Damascus. Only after three years of missionary activity did he journey to Jerusalem to see Peter and James (Gal 1:17-18).

Paul maintains, therefore, that his missionary activity is directly ordained by the Lord and thus as fully authoritative as that of the other apostles. In this, his theology will turn onto a collision course with the later Lukan notion of apostleship in which, strictly speaking, Paul does not qualify for the title "apostle." According to Luke's theology, this title is given only to those who accompanied the earthly Jesus and were eyewitnesses (*martyres*) of Jesus' pre- and post-resurrected life up to the ascension. Consequently, the Damascus experience, which in Paul's letters is an encounter with the risen Jesus and foundational for his apostolic vocation, is not described by Luke as an appearance but as a conversion. Luke ranges Paul's Damascus encounter with Jesus on a level with his later visions, but not in line with earlier appearances of the risen Lord which for Luke must terminate with the ascension. He even construes Paul's calling to be mediated by Ananias. Only in Acts 26:16-17 does his language approach Paul's own understanding of his call in Gal 1:15 ff. and 1 Cor 9:1 ff. as unmediated.[13]

In the context of 1 Cor 9:1 ff., Paul seems pressed to establish his credentials in confrontation with a similar tradition, namely, that appearances of the risen Jesus were limited only to those who, having walked with Jesus and declared themselves his followers, could confirm his post-resurrection identity and be commissioned *directly* by the Lord to the apostolate of preaching. Variations of such a view would even declare that subsequent faith in Jesus' resurrection had been mediated through the testimony of these eyewitnesses.[14]

Now if there is a definite relationship between the preaching of the first eyewitnesses to the appearances of Jesus and subsequent Christian belief, these are not so directly hooked together by Paul as to make their testimony bear the whole weight of either "proving" the resurrection or becoming the sole ground of Christian faith.[15] Jesus' post-resurrection accessibility, which inspired and undergirded the preaching of the select witnesses to the appearances, is in fact the living core of Paul's theology. What is evident from the Damascus experience is that anyone is capable of encountering the risen Lord even though, like Paul, they may never have known Jesus in the flesh. Being among the *first* witnesses of Jesus' appearances, furthermore, did not give any special advantage in the everyday apostolate.[16]

In this regard, the force of the phrase "last of all" (*eschaton de pantōn*) is not so much to indicate that the Lukan tradition of a pre-ascension criterion for being included among the witnesses to Jesus' post-resurrection appearances must be extended to embrace Paul and that with him such appearances are terminated. *Eschaton* can also mean "at last" or "finally" not merely in a chronological sense but, in terms of rank, to those who are least significant. What follows in vs. 9 where Paul calls himself "the least of the apostles" (*ho elachistos tōn apostolōn*) and "unfit to be called an apostle" (*ouk eimi hikanos kaleisthai apostolos*) would seem to support this.[17] The phrase, *eschaton de pantōn*, would indeed be designed to place Paul in the series of special followers of Jesus, privileged to have witnessed to a post-resurrection appearance of Jesus. But, most of all, the phrase leads to the assertion that, even though unworthy of such a calling, Paul was nonetheless *commissioned by Christ himself* to preach to the Gentiles.

Paul's redaction of the resurrection-appearance tradition can, then, be set into the temporal schema which

dominates much of his theology. The *past* event of Jesus'
resurrection and appearances would become the *present* basis
of the community's faith and the commissioning of apostles
and disciples to preach the good news of the salvation
effected by and offered in Christ, and the *future* promise
of new life and resurrection to those who commit themselves
to Christ in faith.[18] This same temporal dialectic gives
a dynamic unity to the entire argument of 1 Cor 15. Jesus'
appearance to Paul founds his mission and inspires not
merely his preaching but the very faith which will make
it possible for the community to affirm the reality of
Christ's resurrection and to nourish their hopes that "in
Christ all shall live" (1 Cor 15:20). For Paul, the resurrection of Jesus is never simply a past occurrence or a
future hope. It began as the central past event of all
history; it focuses on every present moment of the committed believer; and it grounds the Christian future in
which hope for continued renewal of life and the over-
coming of death is assured.[19] Such was the impact of
Paul's encounter with the risen Lord that a sense of the
presence of Jesus dominated the remaining days of his
life and filled him with that enthusiasm and sense of
urgency in preaching the meaning of the passion and resurrection for all ages which become the most compelling
features of his letters. Just what Paul may have "seen"
and understood in that encounter is the subject of the
next sections of this essay.

"Last of All He Appeared to Me": The Sound and Light of Damascus

Definite conclusions about the full "physical" or
"corporeal" nature of Jesus' appearance to Paul must

obviously be hinged to the language whereby Paul describes
that vision. As noted above, Paul adopts an expression
from the early tradition, the aorist passive form *ōphthē*,
to convey the claim that Jesus appeared to an impressive
series of witnesses, building up to his own claim to have
"seen" Jesus. The word *ōphthē* is part of biblical terminology and, as such, ideally suited both to describe a
revelatory experience and to insist on some objectivity
in that experience.[20] It is this same verb, for example,
which emerges in the Septuagint to describe the appearance
of the "angel of the Lord" to Moses in Exodus, "The angel
of the Lord appeared (*ōphthē*) to him" (Ex 3:2). In vs. 4
of this same narrative the subject shifts to the Lord himself who "saw (*eiden*) him go forward to look and called
(*ekalēsen*) from the middle of the bush." God then reveals
his name to Moses and confers on him a specific mission
to his people. He is to tell them that God "appeared"
(*ōptai*) to him. In the priestly version of this same
encounter (Ex 6:2-7), the verb is used to describe the
Lord's manifestation to the patriarchs of old. "God spoke
to Moses and said to him, I am the Lord, who appeared
(*ōphthēn*) to Abraham, Isaac, and Jacob . . . " In each
instance the emphasis in these accounts from Exodus, as in
other biblical uses of the verb, is on the Lord's revelatory initiative. Hence Wilhelm Michaelis concludes that
in the Septaugint *ōphthē* is characteristic of the non-
visual presence of God communicating or revealing himself
to his prophets. The biblical texts stress that God takes
the initiative. There is no direct "seeing" of God, which
would be contrary to Jewish theology anyway, but rather a
manifestation or "vision" in which the auditory aspects of
the revelation predominate.[21]

If Paul is using *ōphthē* in keeping with its religious
sense in the Septuagint, then it would be difficult to
conclude that he was insisting on either a corporeal or
even mental perception of Jesus. Instead, his emphasis
would be on the *revelatory reality* of this encounter.[22]
God has "revealed" himself to Paul. It should be noted,
though, that when a biblical writer uses "see" of God, he
knows he is speaking metaphorically. The question of how
"objectified" was the body of the risen Jesus in his appearances would, because Jesus' case is so unique, be left
deliberately ambiguous. Whether or not Jesus' risen
state was so new and different that the tradition could
only speak metaphorically of his new "incorporeality" must
be left to conjecture. On the other hand, it is highly
improbable that Paul himself regarded his vision as "a
purely internal experience."[23] Aside from the fact that he
aligns his vision with what happened to the "more than five-
hundred brethren at once," Paul also associates his experience with the prophetic vocation. The biblical accounts,
from which Paul draws much of his inspiration, credit
both vision and revelatory audition as palpable basis of
the prophet's conviction that he has indeed encountered
God and received from him a mission.[24] This would tend to
belie any reduction of Paul's experience to a purely
interior or subjective insight.

Because Paul links his having encountered the risen
Lord with the authentication of his apostolate it would
seem likely, both from the sparse references of Gal 1:15 ff.
and the highly elaborated conversion accounts of Acts,
that he was alluding to his Damascus experience. Paul
calls this a "revelation" in Gal 1:16, and he insists in
1 Cor 9:1 that he has seen Jesus--"Have I not seen

(*heoraka*) the Lord Jesus?" Unfortunately, neither assertion gives us much information either about the corporeal
aspects of the appearances of the risen Lord or about the
exact nature of the Pauline vision.

Efforts to supplement these raw claims of the letters
with the Lukan description of Paul's "conversion experience"
in Acts add some dimensions but little clarity to the problem of determining precisely what happened to Paul. Luke's
accounts, moreover, contain no mention of Paul's actually
seeing Jesus' recognizable body, only graphic descriptions
of the sound and light and some of the subsequent events
which turned Paul's entire life around. The Lukan accounts
also contain some minor contradictions with regard to hearing the voice and the effects of the light. In Acts 9:7,
for example, the companions of Paul hear the voice but see
no one. The Acts 22 version mentions in vs. 9 that Paul's
companions perceive the light but cannot hear the voice.
Only Paul is blinded and thrown to the ground. But in
Acts 26:14 both Paul and his troop are knocked to the
ground. Paul alone hears the voice in this version.[25] In
each instance, though, Luke stresses that Paul heard the
voice of the Lord; the vision is that of the blinding
light. The earlier traditions of material employed in
these accounts of Paul's conversion would have to accord
in some way with Paul's own description of the Damascus
experience. It is noteworthy, too, that Luke preserves
the Pauline verb for Jesus' "appearance" in 9:17 and
especially 26:16 where he allows Paul to cite Jesus as
having declared: "I have appeared unto you (*ōphthēn soi*)
to make you a minister and a witness both of those things
which you have seen (*eides*) and of other things which I
shall reveal to you (*ōphthēsomai soi*, literally, "cause
to appear to you"). What Luke adds can be considered

a corroboration and even literary ordering of the Pauline
material if accent is placed on the revelatory nature of
the communication Paul received and which was hidden from
his companions.[26] In short, Luke brings the art of the
storyteller to Paul's unique experience.

If we can prescind from Luke's tendency to downgrade
Paul's status as an apostle,[27] these Lukan texts might tend
to support Paul's bare assertions in 1 Cor 9 and 15. For
Luke, however, Paul's experience is, as we have seen
above,[28] a conversion (the sense of all three accounts) or,
as in Acts 26:19, a "heavenly vision" (*ouranie optasia*),
terms Paul himself avoids using. In fact, Paul is careful
to distinguish the revelatory experience of Damascus from
the ecstatic, revelatory visions of the Lord (*eis optasias
kai apokalypseis Kyriou*) of 2 Cor 12:1. These visions are
considerably distanced from his original encounter with
and direct commissioning by Jesus to apostleship.[29] At
best, even for Paul, they represent only a development in
his spiritual or mystical life. As Walter Künneth has
observed: "Paul experienced ecstatic raptures and knew
himself to be under spiritual guidance; nevertheless he
recognizes the qualitative difference between these experiences and the wholly other, incomparable event of Christ's
appearance on the Damascus road. Here he experiences not
ecstasies, not a prophetic dream with vision and audition,
not a mystical spiritual experience, but a unique encounter
with the neither previously nor subsequently experienced
reality of the Risen One, which was fundamental for his
life."[30] Why that encounter with Jesus was so unique for
Paul's subsequent life can be further explored as we
attempt to analyze the specific nature of the revelation
he alludes to in his letter to the Galatians.

"To Reveal His Son in Me":   Paul's Insight Into the
Eschatological Sonship of Christ

If, in 1 Cor 9:1 and 15:8, Paul has described the
experience in which he came to faith in Christ and, thereby, was commissioned to preach the gospel as "seeing" the
resurrected Lord, he calls that same experience a "revelation" in the earlier Gal 1:16:   "But when God in his good
pleasure who had set me apart (aphorisas) from my mother's
womb and called (kalesas) me through his grace to reveal
his Son in me (apokalypsai ton huion autou en emoi) that I
might preach among the Gentiles, I did not immediately
consult any human being."   This passage is significant for
understanding Paul's experience in that Paul did not feel
constrained to use a visual metaphor to designate what
had happened to him, preferring instead to adopt the concept of "revelation" (apo + kalyptein = to remove from con-
cealment, to unveil) and to associate this manifestation
with God's call (kalesas) to preach (euangelizōmai) among
the Gentiles.   The language here bespeaks, likewise, a
deliberate effort to have his calling considered on a
line with that of Second Isaiah and Jeremiah who, according
to the Hebrew scriptures, had also been destined even
before birth to a God-given mission.[31]
The most crucial phrase of this entire section for
determining the impact on Paul and the insights he derived
from his encounter with Jesus may lie in the cryptic claim
that God had "revealed his Son" in him.   From Paul's allusions to Jesus' sonship in both Romans and Galatians,[32] it
seems that in this revelatory encounter God had granted
Paul the "graced" insight enabling him to recognize that
Jesus was truly God's Son, the expected messiah, now reign-
ing in glory.   The predicate "Son of God" summed up for

Paul both the earthly and heavenly mission of Jesus.

If this was indeed a special "revelation," Paul had,
nonetheless, been himself primed for the experience by
being steeped in Jewish messianic expectations. Specifically, the title "Son of God" can be associated with
Ps 2:7 which speaks of enthroning the Israelite king in
all of his gubernatorial and juridical functions: "The
Lord said to me: 'You are my son, this day have I begotten
you.'" The coronation of the Israelite king has to come
in a direct act from God to the king who thereby receives
the royalty belonging by right to God alone. By the Christian era this psalm had been fully integrated into Jewish
messianic theology. Some strong evidence for such an application of the psalm has been provided by John Allegro in
a published translation of a fragment found among the
Qumran documents in Cave 4. The verses pertinent to our
study read as follows:

    (10) ['And] Yahweh tells you that he will build a house
         for you, and I shall set up your seed after you,
         and I shall establish his royal throne

    (11) [for eve]r. I shall be to him as a father, and
         he will be to me as a son.' He is 'the shoot of
         David' who will arise with the Interpreter of
         the Law, who,

    (12) [. . .] in Zi[on   in the l]ast days; as it is
         written, 'And I shall raise up the tabernacle
         of David that is fallen.' That is the 'taber-
         nacle of David that is fal[len' is he] who will
         arise to save Israel.

From this document,[33] with its obvious messianic-eschatolo-
gical implications, it would appear that "Son of God" was
already the title of a kingly messiah in Jewish thought
contemporary to Paul. This may explain why this Psalm

verse is used in Acts 13:33 (Luke "cites" Paul in this
verse) as an otherwise puzzling scriptural testimony that
God had indeed raised Jesus from the dead. Paul's use of
the concept of royal sonship, expressed so often in his
letters, leads us to wonder whether the "revelation" of
Gal 1:16 was not itself conditioned by and embodied in
existing applications of the Hebrew scriptures to Christ.
In any event, it is clear that the title, "Son of God,"
had important theological implications for Paul who couples
the conferring of divine sonship and subsequent juridical
power with God's raising of Jesus.[34]

Further insight into the implications of the title,
"Son of God," for Paul's comprehending the deeper meaning
of Christ's resurrection can be gained by an examination
of Rom 1:4. Here Paul proclaims that Jesus was "declared
to be Son of God with power (*huiou Theou en dynamei*) according to the Spirit of holiness, by the resurrection from the
dead," and contrasts that with his previous condition as
"seed of David according to the flesh" (*ek spermatos David
kata sarka*). Again, we notice the association of the
resurrection with the act of God's raising of Jesus, thereby establishing him as Son of God in full power.[35] The
conferring of such a title enlightened the early Christians
on the nature not only of Christ's glorification but also
on the manner of his continued presence in the church,
effecting a similar transformation in all united with him
through faith. Joseph Fitzmyer's conclusion on the significance of this passage from Paul's letter to the Romans
is particularly informative:

> The act by which the Father raised Jesus from the
> dead became in Paul's view an endowment of him with
> power as of the resurrection. It is not sufficient
> to explain this verse in terms of some messianic
> enthronement of Jesus. . . . In this passage, then,

Paul seems to be contrasting Jesus as the Son, born into Messianic lineage, with a fuller idea of him as powerful Son 'appointed, installed, constituted' as such as of the Resurrection. Once this is understood, it is easy to grasp how Paul can even come to speak of the risen Jesus as 'the power of God' (1 Cor. 1:24). So endowed at the resurrection, he is, abstractly expressed, the very power of God.[36]

This conclusion would seem to fit not only Pauline christology as developed to the extent manifested in Romans, Galatians and Corinthians but also the essential understanding that the whole complex, resurrection--Son of God in power--messianic Judge, had for Paul. The resurrection would be, then, a confirmation of the more primordial truth that God, true to his promises in raising Jesus, had inaugurated the final times.[37]

This eschatological theme remains a main stream of thought throughout the maze of sub-themes composing 1 Cor 15.[38] Paul here writes of the resurrection of the dead. Because Christ has appeared to him and he has come to recognize Christ as truly God's Son, so the general resurrection of the dead must have already begun. The attribute, "Son of God," applied by Paul to Christ, is as we have seen an indication that Paul saw in Christ's glorification the advent of the final times, for the title implies exaltation of Jesus to the "right hand" of his Father as Judge (2 Cor 5:10; Rom 14:10) and as initiator of the end time (1 Cor 15:20-24; Rom 8:18-19).

With Christ's resurrection as foundation and inspiration, Paul theologizes on the consequences of this for the faith of the Corinthians and for the Christian outlook on life and death. The event is so powerful and encompassing and Christ's role as representative of humanity so unique,[39] that his conquest of death is extended to all Christians who then participate in his "victory." Conversely, Paul

uses the validation of hope in the general resurrection as
"evidence" that Christ has been raised (1 Cor 15:13-16).
Believers will experience a similar resurrection from the
dead in a body transfigured with glory (1 Cor 15:49).
Such is possible because Christ has blunted the sting of
death--"0 death, where is your sting?" (1 Cor 15:55), and
become himself a "living spirit" (*eis pneuma zoopoioun*)
(1 Cor 15:45). In developing these insights Paul uses the
concept of the Christian's new life in the power of Christ's
resurrection to confirm Christian hope in a personal
resurrection, the consequence of that faith in Christ which
Paul's own experience has justified.

In sum, the substance of Pauline eschatology is determined by Paul's own experience of the resurrected Christ.
Paul was convinced that this event, which was decisive
for his personal faith and mission, had given all human
history a totality of meaning and a central point of reference. Jesus could be recognized as the long expected
messiah and as God's own Son, endowed with power over
life and death, and whose presence in the community of
his followers was the guarantee of their call to share in
his glory. Such an eschatological revelation leads us to
wonder whether "the novel and astonishing thing for Paul
was not in the fact that Jesus had risen from the dead but
that . . . the end time had already begun."[40]

Notes

[1]For a clear, balanced description of the problems,
directions, and validity of contemporary "resurrection,"
see Raymond Brown, *The Virginal Conception and Bodily
Resurrection of Jesus* (New York: Paulist Press, 1973),
pp. 70 ff.

[2]The thesis that the formula stems from an Aramaic
speaking, Jewish community in Palestine has been defended
by Joachim Jeremias who cites as evidence the *parallelismus
membrorum*, the absence or particles, the independence from
the LXX of *hyper tōn hamartiōn hemōn*, the use of the adversative *kai* at the beginning of the third line, the position
of an ordinal number after the noun in *tē hēmera tē tritē*,
and the use of the word *ōphthē* instead of the more natural
ephanē which is to be explained by the fact that the Hebrew
nir'ah and Aramaic *'ithame* have the double meaning "he
was seen" and "he appeared"; and the introduction of the
logical subject in the dative after a passive verb,
instead of *hypo* with the genitive. See *The Eucharistic
Words of Jesus* (New York: Charles Scribner's Sons, 1966),
pp. 101-05. This argument, however, has been severely
criticized by Hans Conzelmann in his essay, "On the
Analysis of the Confessional Formula in 1 Corinthians 15:
3-5," *Interpretation*20 (1966), pp. 15-24. Conzelmann points
out that the *parallelismus membrorum* "cannot be a proof
for the original language. It can only indicate that the
tradition of Jewish style controlled the material" (p. 18).
After denying that the *kai* at the beginning of the third
line was adversative or that such could prove a Semitic
original, Conzelmann also attacks Jeremias' argument from
the word order of *tē hēmera tē tritē*. "But it is first of

all," he states, "genuine Greek, and in addition to that, traditional in early Christian-Greek texts" (p. 20). He likewise disputes Jeremias' conclusions concerning *ōphthē Kēpha*: "the recourse to the Semitic usage is not necessary. The usage of the dative with the passive form does not relate to a Semitic language" (p. 20). Finally, he observes that the phrase *kata tas graphas* has no Semitic equivalent. His conclusion is that the original language must have been Greek. Reginald Fuller draws the safer conclusion, "That the tradition as Paul received it was originally Palestinian, but that it has subsequently passed through a Hellenistic Jewish milieu, and that it was this Hellenized form that Paul received." *The Formation of the Resurrection Narratives* (New York: Macmillan, 1971), p. 11.

[3]Jacob Kremer, for example, states that the original formula must have extended at least to vs. 5. The *ōphthē* would, he insists, need a declaration of the persons to whom Christ appeared. Both in Luke 24:34 and in the LXX, he asserts, the naming of those who received the vision is an important part of the tradition. Kremer lists vs. 7 as also certainly pre-Pauline although probably later than the original formula of 3b-5. He bases his argument on the careful parallel of vs. 7 with vs. 5. See *Das älteste Zeugnis von der Auferstehung Christi* (Stuttgart: Verlag katholisches Bibelwerk, 1967), p. 28. Fuller would extend the original pre-Pauline tradition to include vss. 5b-6a and 7. Fuller adopts the thesis of Ulrich Wilckens that Paul has combined four independent traditions, each introduced by *hoti*. See *op. cit.*, pp. 13-14.

[4]Against Fuller and Wilckens, Brown sees as more than coincidental the fact "that four independent formulas would have resulted in the careful balance of alternating

length now found in the "that"clauses of 1 Cor 15:3-5.
See *op. cit.*, p. 83.

[5]We will argue in this paper that it is possible to
read 1 Cor 15 as a whole in which Paul's insistence on his
having seen (*ōphthē*) the Lord establishes his apostolic
credentials and lends credence to his conclusions on the
future general resurrection to occur in Christ. For a
more extensive coverage of the possible inner logic of
Paul's arrangement of the traditional material, we refer
the reader to Raymond Brown, *op. cit.*, pp. 94-96 and
Reginald Fuller, *op. cit.*, pp. 34-48.

[6]We will consider the possible Septuagintal origins
of this phrase below. See notes 10, 20, 21. It should be
noted here, however, that the form *ōphthē*, though an
aorist passive, can have the force of a deponent form when
used with the dative. Hence the active voice translation,
"he appeared." This translates the niphal form of the
Hebrew verb *ra'ah* ("to see") with *1^e* ("to").

[7]Karl H. Rengstorf, *Die Auferstehung Jesu: Form,
Art und Sinn der urchristlichen Osterbotschaft* (Witten,
1960), p. 58, cited by Willi Marxsen, "The Resurrection
of Jesus as a Historical and Theological Problem," (trans.
by Dorothea Barton) in C. F. D. Moule, *The Significance of
the Message of the Resurrection for Faith in Jesus Christ*
(London: SCM Press, 1968), p. 28.

[8]Fuller, *op. cit.*, pp. 28-29. On the specific scriptural references possibly alluded to in the claim that
"Christ died for our sins according to the scriptures"
and "was raised on the third day according to the scriptures," see Karl Lehmann, *Auferweckt am dritten Tag nach
der Schrift* (Freiburg: Herder, 1968), esp. pp. 242 ff.

See also Kremer, *op. cit.*, pp. 31-36, 52-54.

[9]Fuller, *op. cit.*, p. 29.

[10]That such is not necessarily to be concluded has been demonstrated in the careful analysis of this form in a lengthy article by Wilhelm Michaelis. See "*horaō*," *Theological Dictionary of the New Testament* V. V (Grand Rapids: Eerdmans, 1967), esp. pp. 342 ff. Michaelis writes that in the intransitive passive use, the verb refers "only seldom to perception with the eye." See also next note.

[11]Hence Raymond Brown has pointed out: "It is dubious, however, how much of the OT usage really refers to non-physical sight. When, for instance, Gen 12:7 records that God appeared to Abraham, the author may be thinking of God's appearing in a human form, precisely the form in which he could be seen by the eye of man." See *op. cit.*, p. 90; also notes 20 and 21 below.

[12]This redactional motive has been most strongly asserted by Ulrich Wilckens who writes: "The context of the three passages in which Paul explicitly mentions what had happened to him show unambiguously that he at least experienced his own *calling* and authorization as an apostle in seeing the risen Christ. . . . Since his apostolate involved a special personal mission to preach to the Gentiles, he had an obvious reason for laying special emphasis on his own legitimation as an apostle, by contrast to the generally recognized apostolic authority of those who were called before him" (1 Cor 15:8-10). See "The Tradition-History of the Resurrection of Jesus" (trans. by R. A. Wilson), in Moule, *op. cit.*, p. 59. Wilkens' argument is less than convincing when he tries

to deduce from Paul's motives the conclusion that the others listed by Paul in vss 5-7 considered the appearances of Jesus to them as having the same structure and meaning as the appearance to Paul.

[13]See Fuller, *op. cit.*, pp. 45-46; and Xavier Léon-Dufour, *Resurrection and the Message of Easter* (New York: Holt, Rinehart & Winston, 1975), pp. 72-74.

[14]Peter C. Hodgson calls it a "fundamental misinterpretation of the appearances" to argue that they "were limited to the immediate disciples of Jesus, i.e., to those who had known Jesus as an historical figure and were in a position to confirm the identity of the one seen. As such, they are claimed to be a strictly past event although enormously important, since subsequent faith in the resurrection is based on the testimony of those eye-witnesses to the Risen One and is maintained by the slender thread of continuity with those original witnesses." This would, he contends, reduce the appearances to a *past* "proof" of the resurrection. Hodgson correctly sets the focus of the resurrection in the present, what he calls "the coming-to-faith and being-sent-to-mission of the community on the basis of an encounter with the risen Jesus." See *Jesus--Word and Presence: An Essay in Christology* (Philadelphia: Fortress Press, 1971), pp. 225-26.

[15]Such would be the simplistic argument of Gerhard Delling who maintains that "even Paul derives the gospel of the raising of Jesus from the statements of such witnesses as Peter, James, the twelve etc. (1 Cor 15:5-7). At a very early stage this testimony was handed down through the links in a chain of tradition." See "The Significance of the Resurrection of Jesus for Faith in Jesus Christ," in Moule, *op. cit.*, pp. 103-04. Given

the fact that Paul did preach the tradition as it was
handed down to him (the gist of 1 Cor 15:3a), this tradition had to be corroborated in his personal experience,
as the descriptions of his revelatory encounter with the
Lord would seem to indicate.

[16]See Paul's argument in 1 Cor 1:11-17. See also
Gerhard Koch, *Die Auferstehung Jesu von Nazareth* (Tübingen:
J. C. B. Mohr, 1965), pp. 195-96.

[17]Contra C. Freeman Sleeper who insists that "Paul
shares with Luke the conviction that there was a closed
period of time following the crucifixion when the risen
Christ encountered his followers. In fact, if not in principle, the apostolic office is a unique one, limited to
the first generation after the death of Christ. Paul
differs from Luke in two respects: for him the period
is long enough so that he himself is included among the
list of resurrection appearances; and he does not identify
the event which closes the period as the ascension." See
"Pentecost and Resurrection," *Journal of Biblical Literature* 84 (1965), p. 396. Against this conclusion by
Sleeper, which is shared by many exegetes, see especially
Hodgson, *op. cit.*, pp. 226-27. See also the analysis of
the expression *eschaton* in W. F. Arndt and F. W. Gingrich,
*A Greek-English Lexicon of the New Testament and Other
Early Christian Literature* (Chicago: University of Chicago
Press, 1957), pp. 313-14.

[18]Hodgson, *op. cit.*, pp. 223-24.

[19]*Ibid.*, pp. 222-23.

[20]Michaelis, *op. cit.*, pp. 324 ff.

[21]*Ibid.*, pp. 330-34.

[22]Fuller, *op. cit.*, p. 31. See also the final section of this essay for a development of the eschatological aspects of this revelatory encounter.

[23]Brown, *op. cit.*, p. 91. Brown's reasoning here appears logical enough: "Nevertheless, the overall evidence does not favor the thesis that Paul was describing a purely internal experience, for he speaks of Jesus' having appeared to more than 500 at once (1 Cor 15:6); and we can scarcely think of synchronized ecstasy. (This observation holds true no matter where Paul got the information about this appearance; for Paul, who himself saw the risen Jesus, found no contradiction in positing that what happened to him could have happened to 500 people at the same time.)" Of course, much of Brown's conclusion here depends on the content Paul himself invests in the word *ōphthē*. Brown seems to recognize this when he follows his statement with the question: "How are we to reconcile a 'sight' that is not necessarily physical and to be seen by all with an appearance that is not purely internal?" (p. 92). He adds that "the idea of sight/appearance in Paul's description of the risen Jesus is just as paradoxical as the idea of a body that is corporeal but spiritual (not *psychikos*). In short, our language of space-time experience breaks down when it is used to describe the eschatological." In acknowledging this eschatological context, Peter Selby suggests that Paul's reference to the five-hundred witnesses would "offer proof not of the raising of Jesus as such, but of the fact that even of those who had seen the risen Lord a number are still alive though some have died, and that the resurrection has not, therefore, brought about the end of all things. For that is yet to come, and the experience of the

'more than five hundred brethren' testifies to the fact
that the resurrection is in part still in the future."
See *Look for the Living: The Corporate Nature of Resurrection Faith* (Philadelphia: Fortress Press, 1976),
p. 110. What is equally as significant in this reference
is the appeal Paul makes to the experience of others.

[24]Gal 1:15-16, for instance contains clear allusions
to both Second Isaiah and Jeremiah. See note 31.

[25]These descrepancies may be due to Luke's reproduc-
ing separate traditions of Paul's conversion.

[26]Fuller concludes very tentatively that Paul's
experience of the risen Jesus probably was in the form of
a vision of light, such as described by Luke in Acts. He
mentions that, although Paul does not describe the "light"
in either Gal 1 or 1 Cor 15, he does make a very clear
allusion to such a "light" in 2 Cor 4:6--"For it is the
God who said, 'Let light shine out of darkness,' who has
shone in our hearts to give the light of the knowledge of
God in the face of Christ." See *op. cit.*, p. 47. On the
difference between the presentation of Paul's experience
at Damascus by Luke and by Paul himself, see Gerhard
Lohfink, *Paulus vor Damaskus* (Stuttgart: Verlag katholisches
Bibelwerk, 1965), pp. 41-91. See also Dufour, *op. cit.*,
pp. 72-76. Dufour detects a three-fold structure in Luke's
description of Paul's conversion which, in Luke's presentation, parallels a similar structure in the call of
Abraham (Gen 22), of Jacob (Gen 46), and Moses (Ex 3).

[27]See Fuller, *op. cit.*, pp. 45-48.

[28]See note 13 above.

[29]See Kremer, *op. cit.*, p. 59.

[30]Walter Künneth, *The Theology of the Resurrection* (London: SCM Press, 1965), p. 84.

[31]That Paul understands his calling to be like that of Second Isaiah and Jeremiah would seem to be evident from Gal 1:15-16 where Paul links citations from the song of the missionary Servant of Yahweh in an effort to explain the nature of God's revelatory encounter with him. Specifically, there is reference to the calling from his "mother's womb" (Isa 49:1); to the glory given by "my servant" (Isa 49:3); and to the mission to the nations--"I have set you as a light to the nations" (Isa 49:6). Dufour agrees with Lucien Cerfaux that Paul was only indirectly inspired by Jer 1:5 ("Before I formed you in the womb I knew you, and before you were born I consecrated you; I appointed you a prophet to the nations"), citing as evidence the fact that the text from Jeremiah does not contain the crucial expression "called" (*kaleō*) or the positive aspects of "light" and "salvation" of Paul's evangelization mission. Although this latter omission is not all that conclusive, it does seem likely that Paul refers to Isa 49 which, in turn, was imspired by Jer 1:5. See Dufour, *op. cit.*, p. 49. For a further explanation of how Paul relates this "revelation" to his calling to apostleship, see Franz Mussner, *Der Galaterbrief* (Freiburg: Herder, 1974), pp. 81 ff. Lohfink shows how Luke too in Acts 26:16-18, builds a mosaic of citations from Jeremiah, Exechiel, and Second Isaiah, to explain the prophetic nature of Paul's post-conversion mission to the Gentiles. See Lohfink, *op. cit.*, pp. 60-64.

[32]See especially Rom 1:3-4; 5:10; and Gal 2:20, 4:4.

[33]John M. Allegro, *Qumran Cave 4. I (4Q 158 - 4Q 186)* (Oxford: Clarendon Press, 1968). Allegro had published an earlier version of this fragment (4Q Florilegium, Col 1, 1. 10;13) in his article, "Fragments of a Qumran Scroll of Eschatological Midrāsim," *Journal of Biblical Literature* 77 (1958), p. 358.

[34]See Max Brändle, "Zur urchristlichen Verständnis der Auferstehung Jesu," *Orientierung* 31 (1967), pp. 69-70.

[35]Commenting on the passage, Brändle has written: "Were it meant that the human nature of the Son of God is established in power and Lordship, the apposition 'according to the flesh' would stand where in Romans 'according to the Holy Spirit' now stands . . . The contrast: according to the flesh--according to the Holy Spirit envisions not the static difference of natures, but rather the opposition between the conditions of this world and those of the coming world, between the transitory and the eternal, between humiliation and glorification." Brändle's analysis here is aimed at avoiding the impasse which arises when the dogmatic affirmation of Jesus' pre-existence is seen to conflict with the scriptural affirmation that power was *conferred* on him. See *op. cit.*,

[36]Joseph A. Fitzmyer,"'To Know Him and the Power of His Resurrection' (Phil 3.10)," *Mélanges Bibliques en hommage au R. P. Béda Rigaux* (Gembloux: J. Duculot, 1970), pp. 417-18.

[37]Brändle, *op. cit.*, pp. 69-70.

[38]On this unifying theme, H. W. Boers notes that, "Paul was writing about the concluding events of this eon . . . that the resurrection of Christ was

included as the first of these events. The claim of
apocalypticism in I Corinthians 15 is a claim for the
history of Jesus, beginning with his resurrection from
death and ending with his handing the kingdom over to
God the Father, in the sense that this particular history initiates and concludes the end of the present
history. It is not a claim for a *continuing* history.
The claim of apocalypticism in I Corinthians 15 is a
claim for the history of Jesus as eschatology." See
"Apocalyptic Eschatology in I Corinthians 15," *Interpretation* 21 (1967), p. 55. Boers' argument here is, of
course, conditioned by his understanding of the Pauline
notion of "history." Has "history" come to an end for
Paul or will it continue only precariously until the
eschatological period inaugurated by Christ's resurrection achieves its full promise? While the context of
1 Cor 15 is eschatological, nonetheless the fundamental
affirmations of Paul about the significance of the resurrection made it possible for him to adjust his preaching
to the obvious fact that history continued to unfold
with important repercussions for the faith of the community. On this adjustment, not only for Paul but for
Christian theology in general, see especially the section,"The Problem of Eschatology," in Peter Selby, *op.
cit.*, pp. 142 ff.

[39] He is called the "first fruits of those who
have fallen asleep" (1 Cor 15:20); "the last Adam" (vs.
45); and "the second man" (vs. 47).

[40] Brändle, *op. cit.*, p. 69.

RECENT LITERATURE ON THE TRIAL NARRATIVES
OF THE FOUR GOSPELS

Gerard S. Sloyan

In autumn 1973, I published a monograph on the
narratives of the trial of Jesus in the four gospels.[1]
It contained a report of the major recent scholarly
activity regarding the twofold appearance of Jesus before
Jewish and Roman authority described there. The book's
attempt to incorporate dependable writing on the question
up to the time of the completion of the manuscript in
1972, was augmented by the "Select Bibliography on the
Passion and Trial of Jesus" provided by the book's editor,
John Reumann.[2] Professor Reumann dated his selections
from 1961, the year of publication of Bruce Metzger's
Index to Periodical Literature to Christ and the Gospels.[3]
Jesus on Trial went on the assumption that each
evangelist had his own religious and social outlook and
literary style. Besides writing from oral and written
sources (individual traditions developed for catecheti-
cal and liturgical purposes, hypothetical sources no
longer available such as Q, and after Mark, the other
gospels), each wrote from a certain apologetic, theological, and polemical standpoint.
At the outset, I had hoped to write a book that
would adopt a thoroughgoing redactional-critical point
of view. Two difficulties asserted themselves fairly
immediately. Even though the 19th and early 20th-
century literature which thought that the only substantive question about Jesus' juridical process(es) was,

"What really happened?" could be set aside as misguided,
since the evangelists were not demonstrably concerned
with it, the sifting of historical reminiscences from
redactional activity proved an unavoidable challenge.
Not only was it basic to both the modern temper and the
announced ecumenical concerns of the book, it lay beneath
any inquiry into the evangelists' compositional or redactional activity. Or so I thought. I now think that the
step from traditional materials back to historical reminiscences is almost impossible to make, except for the
basic historical realities.

Secondly, the conviction that the key to the interpretation of the trial narratives lay in an analysis of
the redactional technique of each evangelist could not
hide the fact that, by 1972, relatively little work had
been done in that field. The great bulk of research
was literary-historical in orientation (Kilpatrick,
Winter, Burkill, Blinzler, Brandon, Catchpole). Lamar
Cope points out that Cadbury knew fifty years ago, in
The Making of Luke-Acts, that the primary factors in
composition were: "accessible materials, conventional
media of thought and expression, individuality, and the
author's conscious purpose."[4] Lohmeyer (1936)[5] and R. H.
Lightfoot (1934, 1938)[6] were attentive to geography and
structure in Mark as a means of entry into his creative
theology. Obviously the main thrust of redaction criticism did not therefore begin with Conzelmann on Luke
(1953), Marxsen on Mark (1956), or Trilling (1959)/
Bornkamm, Barth, Held (1960) on Matthew,[7] the founding
scholars usually named. At the same time, Donahue's
University of Chicago dissertation of the trial narrative in Mark[8] was not yet out at the time my book was

published (although he kindly gave me the data on it for
the bibliography). Schneider on Luke's narrative of
Jesus before the council[9] and Schreiber on Mark's passion
narrative[10] were already available, as was Linnemann's
collection of studies on the story of the passion.[11]
Schneider's summary account of the tradition history of
the passion narrative in the synoptics appeared before
my book, but I came upon it only afterward.[12]

The main problem appeared to be to establish a
starting point: What is Mark's composition and what is
the tradition he worked with in the trial narratives
(14:53-65; 15:1-20)? *Jesus on Trial* began with a favorable assumption regarding Vincent Taylor's older Semitic
passion account B, arrived at on stylistic grounds, inter-
woven with a straightforward narrative of the suffering
of Jesus, account A.[13] Despite my reservations regarding
the theory, I was convinced that the night trial before
the high priest was an example of Mark's sandwich-
structure or inclusion technique. This meant that it
was composed by him as a christological confession to
establish a contrast with the denial of Peter, within
which it was intentionally set. I was further committed
to the daybreak hearing before Pilate (Mark 15:2) as
the sole historical reminiscence about a true juridical
process; but still bound by the theory going back to
Kähler and Dibelius of a basic pre-Markan passion
source[14] (identified from Dibelius and Bultmann as 14:
1-2; 25-26; 43; 50-54; 65-72; 15:1-5; 15b; 21; 25-26;
34; 37). I recorded Linnemann's challenge to this source
(p. 44, n. 12), which held that Mark was the first one
to work up fragments of the tradition and put them in
sequence, but I did not let it dislodge the conventional

wisdom on the question.

In brief, then, I reported on a redactional-critical treatment of all four trial narratives that was just beginning to be done. This essay provides the opportunity to tell where things stand in 1978, and as part of that to eliminate the problem of historicity almost entirely.

I say that because, as regards the trial narratives proper, their history from the first recorded traditions to their present state seems irrecoverable. It is clear that, since Rome condemned Jesus to death, Pilate would have had to pass sentence, but the only certain echo of that fact occurs in Mark 15:15, "He handed him over to be crucified," and possibly 14:53a, "Then they led Jesus off to the high priest," high priest standing for some sort of Jewish authority. Some think that Mark composed his Jewish trial narrative in imitation of the Roman one for apologetic reasons and to involve Jews in the death of Jesus.[15] There seem to be better reasons than that, however, for his setting the confrontation between Jesus and Jewish authority in the form of a trial, as we shall see. While opposition to Jesus by Jewish authority during his public career is in all probability based on historical reminiscence, it has not contributed anything that can be established with certainty to the night trial of Mark or to his statement that the "whole council held a consultation as soon as it was morning . . . and delivered him to Pilate" (15:1ab). The redaction history of Mark's trial narrative takes us back to some traditional elements, to be sure, but there are no compelling reasons to call them historical reminiscences since all can be explained on other grounds. The Mark-Matthew trial narrative seems

to be exclusively a Markan composition, to which Matthew
has added certain elements (e.g., the name of Caiaphas;
the elimination of "all the chief priests," Matt 26:57;
the addition of the echo of a consummation, "to see the
end," vs. 58). Matthew has likewise added the requirement of the Law, "at least two false witnesses" (vs. 60)
and changed Mark's perhaps embarrassing, because unusual,
"Son of the Blessed" to "Son of God" (vs. 63) = Mark 14:
61). Overall, however, Matthew edits a narrative that
Mark composed. Similarly, Luke[16] and John[17] both seem
to possess Mark's trial narrative, even though a case
can be made, as we shall see below, for a non-Markan
passion narrative possessed by the third evangelist.

Redaction criticism is generally defined, with
Perrin, as the study of the "theological motivation of
an author as this is revealed in the collection, arrangement, editing and modification of traditional material
or the creation of new forms within the traditions of
early Christianity."[18] In this definition, "theological"
describes the religious motifs and typologies that determine the evangelists' overall literary performance.
"Redaction criticism" is an umbrella term that includes
creative composition and adaptation of traditional materials to the evangelist's purpose. While it is possible
to distinguish tradition from redaction (by identifying
the author's stylistic, thematic, and vocabulary characteristics as betraying his redactive hand), this can
never be done with absolute certainty. Distinguishing
a free composition of the evangelist from his redactive
activity is nearly impossible in Mark, whose traditional
materials we cannot cross-check as we can those of the
other synoptics (and occasionally John). At the same

time, it should be evident why the history of the tradition that ends in the form of Mark's gospel is the
most important question of all.

Finally, "traditional materials" are by no means
synonymous with historical reminiscences. Thus, it was
probably traditional for decades to tell stories about
Jesus in his last days as a "suffering just one" on the
model of Pss 22 or 69, or as someone whom false and lying
witnesses had testified against, because of the statements found in Pss 27:12; 35:11; 109:2, without there
being any solid recollection in the community of what
happened to him once he was apprehended. To strip away
redaction from tradition, even where it seems possible,
would only reveal the traditional ways in which the
trial story was told before Mark wrote his gospel.

Critically controlled methods must govern the selection of redactional material, not just the identification
of seams, summaries, and theoretical insertions into
earlier traditions, as Cope has pointed out.[19] The
author's overall purposes and ideas need to be discovered.
"An adequate picture of the work of a gospel writer must
be broader than a resume of his theological biases. It
must encompass something of his literary craft and of
his historical situation as they are revealed in the
gospel."[20] Yet the analytical task precedes the syn-
thetic one, in that "the author's hand must be traced
with great care before any comments can be made about
his overall purposes, theology, and historical situation."[21] Cope, who inclines to the priority of Matthew,
is right in issuing the warning that the redaction
critic is derelict who accepts the findings of a source
critic and lets him/her do the work the redactionist

should do. Finally, he is helpful in reminding us of
the importance of a careful linear reading of a particular gospel in a field where side reference to the synoptic parallels has reigned supreme. In other words,
the evidence of a demonstrable logical pattern of organization must be collected, whether it be the logic of
an argument or the wording of the preceding passage or
the flow of thought which produces the connectives and
provides structure.

The chief outside source used by the evangelists
is the Hebrew scriptures, usually but not always in the
LXX version. Therefore, a valuable key to linear reading is the way an evangelist employs the Bible overall.
Most often he does so in particular pericopes in his
characteristic way; at times he will leave them as he
finds them in his sources.

The Passion Narrative in Mark

Donahue, in the final sections of his last chapter
entitled "The Trial Narrative as Narrative" and "Narrative as Apocalyptic," requires the interpretation of
a gospel in accord with the widely accepted canons
that govern all literature. Having worked with great
care over such Markan stylistic techniques as verbs in
the historic present, *kai* parataxis, and those insertions of a narrative between repeated phrases which are
not mere repetitions but determine the use of the inserted
material (the healing of the hemhorraging woman is the
sole exception of seven intercalations), Donahue asks the
reader to view Mark's trial narrative as a piece of narrative apocalypse, which the whole gospel likewise is.[22]

"Mark composes a trial of Jesus precisely as trial to meet the experiences and demands of the community for which he is writing, a community caught up in the civil strife and trials in the years during and immediately following the Jewish war."[23]

Looking at Donahue more closely, we find that in terms of language and style, the trial scene in Mark (14:53-72) is from the same hand as the rest of the gospel: "it is not simply a piece of unredacted tradition taken over by Mark with little editorial activity."[24] The trial scene is moreover an example of the recognized Markan compositional technique of intercalation. The other examples are: 3:20 f. [intercalation 22-30] 31-35, the Beelzebub controversy; 5:21-24 [25-34] 35-43, the woman who touched Jesus' garment; 6:7-13 [14-29] 30-32, the death of the Baptist; 11:12-14 [15-29] 20-26, the temple cleansing; 14:1 f. [3-9] 10 f., the anointing at Bethany; 14:10 f. [12-16] 17-21 [22-25], the supper and the betrayal, a "double sandwich"; and 14:54 [55-65] 66-72, the night trial. Only in the second case above is there no use of the framing to inculcate teaching on discipleship. The night trial is not simply, therefore, a piece of material which Mark found in the traditions that employed Isa 53, Pss 27 and 35 in order to see in Jesus an innocent sufferer before unjust accusers (not an atoning suffering servant; that development came later). Coupling these traditions with a historical tradition that dealt with the leading away of Jesus to his condemnation and death (*apegagon*, 14:53a), Mark gave to the narrative its formality as a trial.[25] The verses that do this, on the basis of language and style (*Kai anastas*, vs. 60; *epērotēsen*, ibid.; *esiōpa*, vs. 61;

palin, ibid.; not, however Jesus' silence before his
accusers, vs. 61; 15:4, which seems to have been in the
tradition), show the strongest convergence of Markan
characteristics.[26]

Donahue suggests that Mark inserted into the pre-
Markan apologetic tradition of false witnesses (vss. 56-
57) a traditional saying of Jesus about destroying the
temple that had nothing to do with truth or falsity (vs.
58), then altered the tradition on false witnesses to
"witnesses not in agreement" (vs. 59).[27] As to this saying about temple destruction (Mark uses the traditional
naos here, not his redactive *hieron*) and the substitution
of the nascent community as a temple "not built with
hands," that (for Donahue) is Mark's creation. "All previous attempts to suggest a prior form to the saying presuppose that, while two-part, it is, nonetheless, a unified saying."[28] The unity of the saying in its chiastic
structure seems, however, to be the work of Mark. While
there existed in early Christianity a stream of tradition that attributed to Jesus apocalyptic predictions
against the temple and the city (cf. Mark 13:2; 15:29 =
Matt 27:39; Acts 6:14; John 2:19, in the contexts of the
trial of Jesus, the trial of Stephen, and the temple
cleansing, with rebuilding "in three days" a feature of
all but Acts), Mark in recording it appended to it a
second traditional saying on the communal and eschatological temple, the community as a substitute for the
destroyed temple. He is familiar with the Hellenistic-
Jewish commonplace of his day, a "temple not built with
hands," meaning spiritual as opposed to physical (cf.
Acts 7:48; 17:24; Eph 2:11; Heb 9:24). Philo had meant
by it a heavenly archetype as contrasted with the temple

in Jerusalem. Mark is probably contrasting the present
reality of the Jerusalem temple with the future one of
the eschatological community.[29]

The temple saying of the trial narrative is found
in close conjunction with the resolution of the Sanhedrin
to kill Jesus (14:55). In four other places in Mark there
is a similar reference to his destruction: 3:6; 11:18;
12:12; 14:1b. Donahue examines all but the first carefully because in the final four, including 14:55, mention of arresting or killing him occurs in a context of
the opposition of Jesus to the Jerusalem cult or temple,
which is identical with the city for Mark.[30] Mark 11:1-
27 is a unit which shows considerable Markan redaction
of an anti-Temple sort, culminating in the temple discourse 11:28-12:44. Of this, 11:27-12:12 which features
the authority (*exousia*) of Jesus is the midpiece, hence
of central importance to Mark. Mark has provided the
Temple cleansing (11:15-18) as the introduction to the
justification of Jesus' authority ("these things," vs.
28 = immediately preceding activity of Jesus, not his
teaching in general). The debate on Jesus' *exousia* (11:
27-33) vindicates his anti-temple activity (1-27), which
in turn is responsible for the mounting opposition to
him. Similarly, Mark inserts the parable of the tenants
here and adds a citation from Ps 118:22 f. (12:10 ff.)
to continue the anti-cult theme. Mark, by the setting
and content of the allegory, directs it against the Sanhedrin.

Donahue thinks that the use made of Ps 118:22 f.
here stands midway between its use in Acts (4:11) as part
of a passion apologetic and its later developed reference to Christ as the cornerstone of the "spiritual house"

(1 Pt 2:5) which the Christians are to become. Verses
9-10 underscore the substitution of kingdom for temple
(*allois*, 12:9). In Mark's setting, the leaders (11:27)
fail to recognize that Jesus has brought the role of the
temple to a close (12:11 f.). Finally, Mark provides
Jesus' eschatological discourse of chap. 13 (delivered
on the Mount of Olives, opposite the temple mount, vs. 3)
as preliminary to the decision of the leaders to arrest
and kill him (14:1). The central theme of that discourse
seems to be a polemic against a false eschatology in
Mark's day which would join the arrival of the parousia
to the destruction of the temple. False messiahs are
being proclaimed (13:21 f.); the temple has lost its significance: it is now the seat of evil powers (vs. 14).
The coming of the Son of Man, a future event (13:26),
is the central reality for the new community. In light
of all these considerations, ample preparation has been
made by Mark for appending 14:58b to 58a.

The destruction of "this temple" by Jesus is part
of the extant tradition. The replacement of it by another
not made by human hands, the end-time community of Christians, is equally part of Mark's conviction. He puts it
forward to strengthen the faith of a community that has
seen the temple destroyed. False teachers are proclaim-
ing that the end-time has arrived. Mark states, in 14:
58b that it has arrived as hope; the community is the
sign of it. As reality, it will arrive only with the
coming of the Son of Man in glory (13:26). The tradition
behind 14:56, 57 was that witnesses against Jesus had
testified falsely, based on Pss 27:12 and 35:11 in the
LXX. Mark in saying that their testimony "did not agree"
(or "was inadequate," vss. 56, 59) not only softened the

tradition but left the truth of the charge an open question. He inserted a chiastic saying of Jesus of his own composition which he meant to be true: the new community would replace the destroyed temple.[31] He makes a similar insertion, of even greater importance, by bringing to a close Jesus' silence on the question of his being the messiah (the "messianic secret"), which Mark himself created, with the response he has Jesus make to the high priest's question (vss. 61-62). In that response the most important christological titles of Mark's gospel are brought together: Christ, Son of God [the Blessed], and Son of Man. The last of these is used in the trial scene to "interpret and give content to Son of God."[32] When Jesus answers the high priest, "I am," the affirmation has as its content the saying of vs. 62 that follows.

The future Son of Man sayings of Mark 8:28, 13:26, and 14:62 are marked by an apocalyptic imagery which the future sayings of the Q tradition are devoid of (cf. Luke 11:30; 12:8; 12:40; 17:24; 17:26; 17:30, none of which is properly a "coming" saying). The parousia or "coming" sayings of Mark have been thought by Bultmann, Tödt, Manson, and others to be part of the earliest level of tradition. Donahue finds, however, that there was no such fixed group of apocalyptic sayings available to Mark; that while there are texts in the New Testament that contain apocalyptic imagery they have no reference to Son of Man (e.g., 1 Thess 1:10; 3:13; 4:16; 2 Thess 1:7); and that it was Mark who creatively merged the two streams of tradition in 8:38, 13:26, and 14:62, the last of which in the trial scene is climactic. Jesus' answer to the high priest is the church's confession, through

Mark, that suffering ("Son of Man"), judgment ("seated
at the right of Power"), and salvation of the elect
("coming with the clouds of heaven") are united in the
apocalyptic Christ. The messianic secret is unveiled:
the suffering Jesus is the Christ who will return in
glory to vindicate his chosen ones.

The literature of the last few decades (including
Jesus on Trial) is filled with discussions of the supposed
tension between Ps 110, a royal enthronement psalm, and
Dan 7:13, a vision of future judgment. The former was
thought to connote exaltation/resurrection exclusively,
the latter parousia. This raised the question, which of
the two did Mark intend with his "Son of Man seated at
the right hand . . . and coming with clouds" (vs. 14)?
Donahue sees in the trial scene a midrash on the psalm,
especially vss. 5-7, in which Jesus is seated at the right
hand of the Father while simultaneously victorious
over enemies in whose midst he appears as judge ("he
will execute judgment among the nations," vs. 6). Recourse
to Paul's vision of final judgment in 1 Cor 15:24 f., and
his citation of the risen Jesus as our intercessor in
Rom 8:33 f., both of which depend on Ps 110:1, convinces
Donahue that the psalm is cited in a context larger than
proof of the resurrection only. "There is no tension
between exaltation, judgment, and parousia. . . . In Mark
14:62b the addition of Dan 7:13 and the complex of ideas
associated with it (judgment, rule, giving of kingdom,
cf. 13:26) complements the meaning of Ps 110:1 and creates
a sequence like that of 1 Cor 15:24-25."[33] Donahue's
final statement on the construction of Mark's trial scene
is important:

> By joining the Christological material of 14:62 and
> the temple saying of 14:58 in the trial narrative,

Mark continues the pattern of the eschatological expectation of the return of the Son of Man and the founding of the new community, but he does this in a manner that is less clear than in other sections, and in a manner which leaves the future ambiguous for a community which like the disciples denies Jesus at the moment of greatest crisis.[34]

This fits in well with the conviction that the ending, "for they were afraid" (16:8) underscores the ambiguity, leaving an uncertain community with the sole certitude that will "see" Jesus in a Galilean parousia, "just as he told you" (vs. 7).

Perhaps the best contribution of Donahue is his setting of the trial narrative, in his final chapter, in the context of the Markan community. The designation and purpose of a given gospel is a basic concern of redaction criticism. With Marxsen, R. Pesch, and Kelber, Donahue inclines to a post-70 date for Mark in the wake of the disarray of the temple's destruction, He thinks that Mark chose to compose a trial narrative in Jewish circumstances, not Roman, because his community has undergone trials at the hands of Jewish officials. There is an immediacy to the persecutions described in 13:9-13 that Matthew and Luke back off from. The Markan gospel, in other words, exhorts to fearless witnessing. It has a present policy on martyrdom that the others do not. The scanty evidence we have on the persecutions of Nero (A.D. 54-68) and Domitian (81-96) do not fit the Markan facts, whereas the pogroms against Jews between 66-70 described by Josephus seem to do so.[35] Warring Zealot factions fought for control of the temple in those years, held summary trials, and are even known to have turned an enigmatic figure named Jesus, son of Ananias, over to the governor Albinus (62-64), who had him scourged and

let go.[36] His crime in Zealot eyes was prophetic activity
against the temple, an activity in which the Christians
were clearly implicated. If Donahue's theorizing is
correct, Mark chose the trial form to convey his horta-
tory message in existential terms.

This brings to mind Winter's view that, "Once the
writer [Mark] had conceived of the plan to ascribe the
responsibility for Jesus' death to the ill-will of the
Jewish leaders rather than a clash with Roman authority,
he felt it necessary to show how the animosity of certain
groups had been aroused."[37] Winter's total historical
skepticism about the opposition of Jewish religious
authority to Jesus is not, however, shared by Donahue.
The latter does not take on precise historical questions,
it is true. But in suggesting a Mark who makes the
world in which his readers live intelligible and bearable,
because it imitates the one their master experienced, he
assumed Mark's possession of long-standing traditions
about Jewish opposition to Jesus and his followers.[38]
The phenomenon is not new in 66-70.

Wilcox, along the same lines as Donahue, thinks that
Mark wrote the story of Peter's threefold denial of Jesus
(14:26-31, 66-72), a self-contained unit within which the
night trial is set, to show that the saying of Jesus of
14:27a and 30 ("You will all fall away . . . You will deny
me three times") was fulfilled.[39] Jesus had told his
disciples "all things beforehand" in the apocalyptic
discourse (13:23), that is, his words were preserved so
that their fulfillment could be recognized at the appropriate time. He had proclaimed a time of testing to
come on the whole world, which had in turn been fore-
shadowed in Zechariah (13:7-14:4; see Mark 14:27):
"Strike the shepherd, that the sheep may be scattered."

The story of Peter's denial, despite its appearance as
a vignette, is therefore chiefly about this time of
testing. It is subordinate to the saying of Jesus which
employs Zechariah, and is used for purposes of expound-
ing it. So enormous was the crisis of A.D. 70 that even
Peter, presumably honored as a martyr by the time Mark
wrote, was brought to the test and found wanting. How
much more should Mark's readers be on guard! Wilcox
does not mean to cast doubt on the historicity of a
Petrine denial of Jesus. He seeks to discover the redactional policy of "the Evangelist of his tradition (or
both)" which underlay the anti-Petrine portrayal of this
somewhat artificially told tale. He suggests that 14:31
may contain the key to all: "If I must die with you. . . ."
The *dee* connotes the necessity of a divine design, the
synapothanein the death of believers along with Jesus
in the troubled days that led up to and marked the siege
of Jerusalem.

Werner Kelber's *The Passion in Mark*, a collection
of essays by Norman Perrin and his students subtitled
Studies in Mark 14-16, brings to an English-speaking
readership the fruits of recent German redactional scholarship and some that is original in the United States.[40]
Donahue provides the "Introduction: From Passion Traditions to Passion Narratives," telling the story of the
early insights of Dibelius, Dodd and Taylor, with Barnabas Lindars' *New Testament Apologetic*[41] as a bridge to
the work of Perrin and more recently Linnemann, Schenke,
Schenk, and Dormeyer.[42] He had already incorporated the
available works of Schreiber and Schneider into his dissertation. Donahue contributes one essay on the trial,
"Temple, Trial, and Royal Christology (Mark 14:53-63),"

and Norman Perrin the other, "The High Priest's Question and Jesus' Answer (Mark 14:61-62)." Interestingly, the trial before Pilate is not dealt with in an exegetical essay. Donahue cites Braumann to the effect that the Sanhedrin trial in Mark is "both secondary to its context and modeled on the Roman trial."[43] Perrin mentions it in discussing the idea of Jesus as king, which is introduced in chap. 15 ("For Mark the crucifixion narrative is the narrative of the enthronement of Christ as King")[44] and Kelber compares the conduct of the high priest and Pilate in the twin trials. Kelber concludes that Mark, by his portrayal of the high priest as seeking Jesus' conviction (14:63) and Pilate as "wondering" (15:5, 44), intends to reverse "the conventional model of friend and enemy." The foreign, hostile power suspects priestly envy (15:10) and tries to save Jesus' life.[45]

Donahue's introductory essay cites a series of recent book-length studies which distinguish tradition and redaction in Mark on vocabulary and stylistic grounds (complete with statistical counts), suggesting that an independent and coherent passion narrative prior to Mark is extremely doubtful. Whatever the complex tradition history that led to his gospel, he seems to be the considerable redactor of the following traditional pericopes: the anointing (14:3-9), the passover meal (14:12-25), the prediction of denial (14:26-31), the Sanhedrin trial (14:53-65), and major elements of the crucifixion story (15:20b-41). He appears to both bring them into the narrative and be responsible for their connection. All the major themes of the gospel, especially the conjunction of the sufferings of Jesus with that of Christians (13:9-13; 14:32-42) are made to culminate in

the passion narrative.[46]   Yet Mark is not a mere commen-
tator on tradition. The text in its final form has been
shown by Neirynck to be the product of one creative hand.[47]
This fact sets Donahue against the main thrust of German
Markan scholarship, which looks for a pre-Markan *Vorlage*
in every verse and half-verse. His tendency is to view
Mark as an author and theologian and to turn attention
to the composition and structure of a whole gospel, for
example those strategic places where Son of Man is used
to reinterpret Son of God. Kelber and Weeden have also
done this, following the lead of their teacher Perrin.[48]

Donahue's essay on Mark 14:53-63 in Kelber is a summary of his dissertation. It goes uninfluenced by the
German tendency, continued in Schrenk, Schrenke, and
Dormeyer, to derive Mark's theology primarily from redactional material that is set more or less in dialectical
opposition to the tradition. Donahue notes, in discussing
Jesus' temple saying, that each major anti-temple section of Mark is followed by a notation that the temple
leaders sought to kill Jesus (11:18; 12:12; 14:1).[49]
Mark sees the temple as having lost its meaning to Christians. As to the christological logion of 14:61-62,
the response to the high priest is seen as anticipating
chap 15, where Jesus will be enthroned as King and hailed
as Son of God. Donahue finds Mark pursuing a David theme
for Jesus, in a passion account that parallels that king's
adventures in 2 Sam 15 and 16 fairly closely (ascending
Mt. Olivet with three friends, one of whom threatens
violence; betrayal by an intimate, etc.). He spells out
the royal christology of the entire gospel, not just
that of chap. 15 onward, finding support in the fragment
of the Qumran scroll from Cave 4 which calls some myster-

ious apocalyptic, human figure "Son of God" and "Son
of the Most High." Rather than seeing a muting of a
Hellenistic theme, which is the conventional wisdom on
the point, Donahue finds a heightened Semitic royal christology. From the first exorcisms of Jesus in Mark onward,
he acts in the Jewish tradition, reported by Josephus,
like a king whose kingdom spells the downfall of evil.[50]
In the manner of David he takes food while he is wander-
ing and has not yet established his kingdom.[51] Jesus
is likewise pictured as the anointed king who is being
kept from full possession of his kingdom and locked in
a struggle to obtain it. Mark uses the royal christology motif in 14:62 to provide the bridge between the
temple saying and the christology of the trial. The
trial and death of Jesus are then interpreted as the suffering of the crucified king. The mockery heaped on him
as a false prophet occurs just when his prophecy about
Peter is being fulfilled. In all this, Donahue derives
insights from Donald Duel's 1972 Yale dissertation, which
he calls "the most recent and thorough investigation of
the temple saying."[52]

Perrin examines in Kelber the way the question and
response of the high priest and Jesus (14:61-62) *functions*.
Retrospectively, it marks the formal disclosure of the
messianic secret and is the climax of Mark's christological concerns. Prospectively, it prepares for the
centurion's confession; it likewise interprets Jesus'
crucifixion/resurrection as the enthronement/ascension
of Jesus as Christ and Son of Man; and it anticipates
the parousia. In Mark, risen-life appearances would
have interrupted this flow. Perrin identifies as his
discovery, after a publishing career beginning in 1968 of

basically form-critical work, the way the various Son of
Man passages function in Mark, from the literary-critical
standpoint of all that the evangelist intends.

As to the recent German redactional scholarship
referred to above, chiefly on Mark, there is the 1972
summary of L. Ruppert on Jesus as the suffering just
one,[53] which in turn derives from his much larger study
of this theme in Bible and postbiblical Judaism.[54] The
discovery of the motif of the biblical innocent sufferer
in the passion narratives is not new (e.g., betrayal by
friends, Mark 14:18, 43; Ps 55:14-21; silence before
opponents, Mark 14:61; Pss 38:14-16; 39:10; mockery by
enemies, Mark 15:20, 29; Pss 22:8; 35:19-25; 109:25).
Ruppert's contribution is to trace the adaptations made
of the earlier lamentations in the psalter ("the suffering just one") through the suffering prophet of the
Isaiah servant-songs, then the responses to crises that
overtook Israel in the Maccabean (cf. Dan 11:33-35;
12:1-3) and other end-time oriented periods (cf. 1 QH
2:20-30; 3:37-4:4; 15:14-17; Wis Sol 2:12-20; 5:1-7'
En 104:3). Thus, the evangelist Mark does something
that is already traditional when he portrays Jesus as a
beleaguered righteous sufferer and prophet, in word-
pictures derived from numerous biblical places but notably
the diptych of Wis 2:12-20 and 5:1-7. There the accused
and condemned righteous one, at his death, confronts his
oppressors with assurance, to be numbered finally among
the sons of God. Ruppert concludes that there are enough
authentic sayings of Jesus to establish that he saw in
himself the suffering just one and prophet whose future
exaltation as eschatological Son of Man was assured. His
creative personality so harmonized prophetic and

apocalyptic traditions as to bring forth a self-image of
one whom God would vindicate in the last age. The image
of a vicarious sufferer, however, was a conception of
the early church.[55]

Ludger Schenke's careful study of Mark's passion
narrative from the initial resolve of the chief priests
and scribes to kill Jesus to his arrest in the garden
distinguishes between the pre-Markan tradition and Markan
redaction in these verses.[56] Without citing Ruppert's
researches, Schenke likewise is committed to the motif
of the righteous sufferer underlying Mark. He thinks
that Mark edits the traditions of a Hellenistic Jewish-
Christian community which stresses Jesus' foreknowledge
and divine power, correcting a false christology and
pressing his view of true discipleship in the process.
Schenke's shorter work (which incorporates Ruppert's
findings), entitled "The Crucified Christ," is a literary
and tradition history analysis of Mark 14:53-15:20a,
placed between examinations of 14:32-52 and 15:20b-47.
With respect to the Jewish trial proper, he designates
14:53a, 55-56 60-62a, 63-65 traditional material, to
which Mark has added the redactive 14:53b, 57-59, 62b
and 15:6-15a. In the Roman trial, 15:1, 3-5, 2, 15b,
16-20a are designated as the original pre-Markan stratum.[57] He identifies the major interest of the early
church in the passion and death of Jesus as a dogmatic
one in the crucified messiah from which apologetic and
polemic tendencies are not absent. He hesitates to call
the trial scene simply unhistorical, saying that it is
much easier to declare what lies behind it than what
does not.

Schreiber's brief work on the passion in Mark

reviews the history of form criticism, then gives the
views of Bultmann and Dibelius on the Jewish trial narrative, followed by his own "thoroughgoing redactional
history exegesis."[58] Like several scholars cited above
he thinks that Mark's christology and eschatology determine his redactive activity, also that his composition
may be the chief passion source for John as well as
Matthew and Luke.[59] Schreiber draws on his own extensive earlier investigation of Mark 13 and the crucifixion account in 14:21b-41 for this briefer summary,
which explores only 14:55-64 and 15:42-47.[60] In that
"Theology of Trust" he sees Mark opposing a Gentile
Christian Hellenistic theology by the historicization
of an original apocalyptic portrayal of the crucifixion.
He thinks that Simon of Cyrene and the circle of Stephen,
both of them Hellenist Jews, are the sources for Mark's
crucifixion pericope. Their account is told in the historical present while the second narrative (15:25, 26,
29a, 32c, 33, 34a, 37-38) bears the traces of Jewish
apocalyptic. It is, however, Hellenistic-Jewish and
Gnostic influenced. What is most important about
Schreiber's 1967 work is that he was the first to hold
that Mark composed the original passion narrative, there
having been no continuous pre-Markan *Vorlage*.

W. Schenk, like Schreiber, is interested in Gnostic
influences in a Hellenist church which Mark sets himself to correct.[61] Two traditions preceded Mark, one
in a simple narrative vein, the other apocalyptic.
These were underlain by a "Simon stratum" and a "seven-
hour apocalypse stratum." The strata leading to the
traditions which Mark joined in his crucifixion account
are not far from Schreiber's two. The apocalypticism

(15:25, 26, 29ac, 30, 33, 34a, 37, 38, 39) is false and
Mark sets himself to correct it, starting with the verse
that sets the tone of the entire gospel: "The Son of
Man has not come to be served but to serve--to give his
life in ransom for the many" (10:45). The error of
Mark's Gnostic-tinged apocalyptic opponents is that they
think that with the destruction of the temple they are
living in the new age.

A book of great thoroughness after those above
which study particular pericopes of Mark's passion is
D. Detlev Dormeyer's Münster dissertation of 1974 on the
passion as containing all Markan characteristics.[62] He
finds the researches of Schreiber and Linnemann, among
others, defective on grounds of method, and proceeds
first to a vocabulary-count and style-critical analysis
(with form, genre, and theological criticism presupposed)
of the first thirteen chapters. He then examines rigor-
ously each verse from 14:1 to 16:8, and concludes from
the distinct vocabularies of redaction ("r") and tradition ("t") which he has discovered that there is a three-
level situation in the last three chapters. The actual
gospel text is obviously one of them; Dormeyer designates
this Rmk, the final redaction by Mark. The earlier two
are a hypothetical T (for "tradition"), which was a primitive Christian acts of a martyr, a conflation of pagan
Greek and Jewish literary patterns, and Rs, a secondary
redaction of T. The latter is marked by the addition
of dialogue and sayings of Jesus (e.g., his words to
the woman who anoints him in 14:6 and to the disciples
in 14:23b; the challenge of the high priest in 14:61b).[63]
All three strata are redactions, including T where the
motif of the suffering just one influences the portrait

of the martyr Jesus. Rs modifies T chiefly under the
influence of a christology which views Jesus as Israel's
true messiah and promiser of the coming kingdom, concluding in faith in him as crucified and risen.[64] His enemies
misconstrue all this, his disciples deny him and flee,
while the holy women are fearful. Rmk introduces the
title Son of Man to reinterpret the christology of Rs
and show Jesus as the final judge of all. His words,
meantime, are a new and authoritative Scripture.[65]

With yet another theory, (viz., Dormeyer's), on the
growth of the tradition, culminating in Mark's final
redaction, the hypothesis of a single pre-Markan passion
narrative is in considerable jeopardy. Mark seems to
have brought the tradition of the Sanhedrin trial into
the account, among a half dozen other pericopes. He is
editor, connecter and composer of the entire gospel in
the interests of a single word-picture, both to "present
unbelief graphically" (Conzelmann) and to nurture faith.
All sorts of connected accounts previous to his 14:1-16:8
have been posited, but what emerges clearly is that no
one of them can be demonstrated as having had to exist,
if only because the many "witnesses do not agree."

The Passion Narrative in Matthew

Until the studies of Strecker[66] and Trilling,[67]
there had not been any thoroughgoing explorations of
Matthew's theology on a redactional principle. Trilling
produced a brief essay on the Matthean passion narrative
for a Beuron symposium in 1965, as had Dahl in 1955-56
for *New Testament Studies*, but the field was largely
open until D. Senior published his Leuven dissertation

under Frans Neirynck (1972) in 1975.[68] He emerged from
his investigation convinced that Matthew's passion narrative can be most adequately explained in terms of
direct dependence on the text of Mark. It is consistent
in style and ideas with the rest of his gospel, even
though "there is no single grand design capable of
explaining all of Matthew's significant content changes."[69]
Matthew concentrates on discipleship in dealing with the
denial of Peter (26:69-75), and gentile accession to Jewish
privilege, coupled with Jewish responsibility, in the
Roman trial scene (27:11-26). In both cases, he derives
the intrinsic qualities of his account from Mark. Elsewhere, in what at first seems to be a case of "special
Matthew," Matthew can be seen to be developing themes
and basic material in dependence upon Mark, "highlighting
. . . ideas already inherent in the account."[70] There
are, of course, some passages unique to Matthew (notably
27:3-10, the death of Judas) but they always tie in with
basic themes in Markan parallels (in this case, to Matt
26:14-16 and 27:11 ff.). Senior sees in the incident of
Pilate's wife (27:19) and the dramatic gesture of the
governor in relinquishing judgment (vss. 24 f.), with its
message of Jewish responsibility for the innocent blood
of Jesus, "a natural development of the Markan presentation."[71]

Matthew does not re-write Mark slavishly but uses
him intelligently in support of his major interest, a
heightened christology to which are subordinated discipleship, moral exhortation, and Jewish responsibility
for Jesus' death. It is the latter that is most obviously
at work in the trial narratives, Jewish and Roman. Matthew
starts his passion narrative with Jesus in magisterial

control and first re-groups the members of the Sanhedrin.
He adds to Mark a formal "taking counsel together"
(*synebouleusanto*, 26:4) of the chief priests and elders
(the latter substituted for Mark's scribes, who reappear
in vs. 57), in the palace of the high priest Caiaphas,
whom he names (27:3 and again at 57). He eliminates
Mark's ambiguity about the "many" and the "some" who
bore false witness against Jesus (14:56, 57) by attribut-
ing a search for *pseudomartyrian* to the chief priests
and the whole council, "that they might (*hopōs* in place
of Mark's *eis*) put him to death" (Matt 26:59). Matthew
improves on Mark's style, clarifying and simplifying
him throughout. He seems to posit a parade of false
witnesses until two, under Mosaic law, come forward to
give valid testimony about a temple destruction saying
on which Jesus is found guilty (vss. 60b, 61). This leads
to the messianic proclamation of vss. 63 f. Matthew
changes the temple saying of Mark (14:58) from "I will
destroy" to "I can destroy," and substitutes "the temple"
for Mark's dialectic about one made and not made with
hands, to heighten Jesus' controlled power with regard
to the actual Jerusalem edifice. Senior opts in 14:62
for a single question of Caiaphas connoting amazement
at Jesus' silence, understanding the *ti* as relative and
not interrogative. The formula of adjuration (*ekorkizo
se*, vs. 63) seems to be a Matthean composition for solem-
nity's sake. The response of Jesus to Caiaphas' question, as the latter if framed, is remarkably close to
Peter's confession of Jesus in 16:16, with "son of the
living God" added to Mark, in both places. Jesus'
response (vs. 64 = Mark 14:62) features the phrase *ap'
arti*, "hereafter," probably to signal the completion of

Jesus' work in his death (cf. the similar usage in the vow of abstention at 26:29).[72] Matthew's emphasis in his redaction of Mark is on Jesus' power and authority (26:61) and explicit confession of his messianic identity (26:63 ff.). He underscores the latter by adding the title "Christ" to the taunting of the mockers in the Jewish court to have Jesus prophesy (26:68).

Senior does not follow unequivocally the opinion of D. Catchpole on the significance of the change of Mark's "I am" to "You have said it" (Mark 14:62 = Matt. 26:64). Yet it seems the most balanced view. Catchpole examines the changes made by Matthew in Mark's account of Jesus before Caiaphas, having explored and rejected the evidence alleged for Matthew's possessing any source but Mark for this pericope.[73] He attributes the change "You have said it" (*su eipas*) to a more Semitic idiom in line with the general character of Matthew, but not to a lowering of christology, least of all in this climactic exchange. Rather, Matthew makes Jesus say "Yes" but with the implication that the "more" that follows, the kingly Son of Man saying, is needed for understanding Jesus. Catchpole, against Cullmann, does not see Matthew's inserted *plēn* setting up a contrast between messiah and Son of Man, since in 16:13-23, a heavily redacted passage, the two titles co-exist with ease. In 26:64, *plēn* introduces an explicit defining statement after an earlier one ("You have said it") which declined to state expressly something affirmative that required further definition.

Both accounts conclude with a general hearing of witnesses, Mark 14:55 f. = 26:59-60a. Matthew heightens their alleged falsity (vs. 59), but when it comes to the temple saying he is at pains to make *this* testimony

true and valid at law (cf. Deut. 16:6 f. and 19:15).
Any suggestion that the saying of Jesus is to be included
in the previous false accusations is erased. In fact,
Jesus' hostile attitude to the temple is softened from
his *intent* to destroy to his *power* to do so; a reveren-
tial tone is introduced; the contrast between this temple
and another is removed. Matthew's consecutive, legally
and theologically connected narrative eliminates Jesus'
opposition to the temple but only shows his power in it.
This accords with Matthew's previous version of temple
sayings (12:1-8; 21:10-17) which makes them serve christological ends. Thus, according to Catchpole's 1971
article, Matthew's redaction of 26:60b-64 is in line with
his treatment of temple passages (see 27:40, 43).

Senior, however, does not think Jesus' reply to the
high priest in Matthew is affirmative, but he does think
that the *su legeis* of 27:11 is. He examines at consider-
abl length the changes, both stylistic and grammatical,
made by Matthew in Mark. His chief redactional findings
are that Matthew wishes to make the necessity of choice
between Barabbas and Jesus far clearer than Mark. The
people make a deliberate choice of Barabbas, hence the
Jewish people and their leaders know that what they are
doing "lifts the prerogative of Israel from their hands."[74]
Senior is seemingly untroubled by Matthew's stress on
Jewish responsibility, "While an evident characteristic
of [his] presentation, [it] is ultimately subordinated
to a more fundamental fascination with the majesty of
Jesus."[75] Not for this reason only but for the lack of
a consistent critical viewpoint as he analyzes a myriad
of stylistic changes, Senior does not seem to be the last
one from whom we shall hear about the Matthean redaction.

The Trial Narrative in Luke

Catchpole's 1971 study, *The Trial of Jesus*, held
that the Lukan Sanhedrin hearing (22:66-71) derived from
a source previous to and independent of Mark 14:53b,
55-64; 15:1a, to which it is historically superior.[76] I
espoused the same view, largely on the basis of Taylor's
arguments.[77] Catchpole's work had been preceded by
Gerhard Schneider's of 1969, cited in n. 7 above, which
he came upon late and hence was able to deal with only
in an appendix.[78] Schneider examined Luke 22:54-71 (from
capture of Jesus to the high priest's declaration that
he is guilty from his own lips). His conclusion is that
only 22:63-64, 66-68 (mockery by night in the high priest's
courtyard and a Jewish question and response "when it was
day," in which Jesus is asked if he is the Christ and
Son of God) is special Lukan material.[79] He thinks that
the whole of Peter's denial (22:54-61) is traceable to
Mark of free Lukan redaction, with the hypothetically
possible exception of vss. 55bc, 60d, as is vs. 70, "And
they all said, 'Are you the Son of God, then?' And he
said to them, 'You say that I am.'" A dominant redactional motif is a concern to shield Peter and to lessen
the measure of his shame[80] (although one may question
whether it has this effect). Schneider checks out the
correspondences of John and Luke from Luke 22:54 onward,
which do not include Luke's similarity to Mark, and concludes that the existence of a passion tradition besides
Mark which both drew on is a possibility.

The Passion Narrative in John

The only substantial piece of Johannine redaction

criticism on the passion narrative in recent years is A.
Dauer's 1972 Würzburg dissertation written under Schnack-
enburg.[82] He thinks that an independent tradition underlay John 18:1-19:30 that was not identical with Mark
but was influenced by the synoptic accounts which points
parallel John exactly. "We are dealing here with a
merging of oral and written tradition,"[83] he writes. As
to his theological inquiry, Dauer concludes that John
presents Jesus' sufferings and death as part of his
exaltation and glory.[84] The account begins with the manifestation of divine glory that sends the guards reeling.
Jesus is in complete charge as Lord before the high
priest. His answer to him reveals him as final judge of
the world. The exchange with Pilate is the occasion for
declarations about the world's unbelief, while Jesus'
last word, "It is completed," is a statement of his
victory. Nothing in the passion and death happens
against Jesus' will; all is an act of free obedience to
the Father. John is most indebted to the tradition when
he has events in the passion fulfill prophecy--the cast-
ing of lots for Jesus' clothes, the drinking of vinegar,
the breaking of his legs and piercing of his side. The
evangelist takes this traditional material over because
he views the Bible as a positive source for understanding Christ and has an answer in it for the unbelief of
those he calls "the Jews." Dauer finds a political-
apologetic tendency in John: Jesus and the Christians
are politically innocent. Since "the Jews" denounced
him to the Caesar and he was condemned under this pressure, the guilt lies there. Finally, Jesus' role of
witness to the truth is underscored by the roles assigned
to various players in the passion story--disciples, Mary,

the one whom Jesus loved, his mother. All of these
themes have surfaced in other Johannine studies. Dauer
by his careful vocabulary and redactional study has established both their validity and his right to maintain
them.

Ernst Haenchen wrote on the Johannine passion narratives in 1967 that was translated into English in 1970.[85]
It cannot be classified along with contemporary redaction or composition critical studies. The author shows
an awareness of the influence of Psalm verses like 27:2
and 35:4 on narratives in the fourth gospel such as that
of 18:6. In general, however, his major concern is
what would be historically likely, concluding along the
way that a Jewish trial and soldiery were more probable
than a Roman, the latter having been added to show the
measure of Jesus' power and wisdom. Haenchen thinks
that the Johannine passion narrative had as its goal, not
to awaken the reader's sympathies for Jesus, but to cele-
brate the victor who followed the unswerving cause of
God to his last breath: "the cause of the love of God."

In contrast to Haenchen's view, Hans Conzelmann in
a broad-brushed sketch holds that there is nothing dis-
coverable in the passion narratives that is historical
beyond the fact that Pilate issued a writ of execution
for a death sentence passed by a Jewish court and that
he sentenced Jesus. Conzelmann does not say how he knows
that a Jewish court passed sentence. He reports on the
trial as a piece of "christological tradition scenically
formed (like the scene of Peter's confession)."[86] The
trial before Pilate is to be understood in similar
fashion: it too is without historical basis. In this
essay, written a decade ago, Conzelmann cites little

scholarship except that of Best[87] and an earlier work of
Haenchen.[88] Matthew's passion is a stage on a road that
runs in a straight line to Jesus' enthronement (28:16- 20).
Jesus' "hereafter you will see . . . " (26:64) is verified
in the Church and in the fate of Israel. The Jews are
driven to self-condemnation in the Roman trial of Matthew.
Luke does not dissolve the passion into a series of isolated salvation events, like Matthew. For him, the passion
is the condition for salvation. Before it is consummated,
Jesus reigns by teaching in the temple, thereby establishing the claim of the Church to be the true Israel. In
contrast to Mark, he allows Jesus to be killed precisely
at the passover feast (22:1). Conzelmann's article is a
strange, slapdash performance--correct in the general
positions it takes but without supporting scholarship
except such as the erudite author possesses from memory.

The world of New Testament scholarship can expect,
within the next few years, further studies on the passion
narratives, especially of Luke, on a composition-criticism
principle. Meantime, the studies of the last decade
and especially those done since the completion of *Jesus
on Trial* have been very fruitful. They are an indication of what we may expect as linear rather than lateral
studies on the individual gospel writers multiply.

Notes

[1] Gerard S. Sloyan, *Jesus on Trial: The Development of the Passion Narratives and Their Historical and Ecumenical Implications*, edited with an introduction by John Reumann (Philadelphia: Fortress Press, 1973).

[2] Pp. 136-49. Limitations of space imposed by the publisher as the book reached page-proof stage necessitated an editing down of this bibliography by about one-third of the journal articles.

[3] *New Testament Tools and Studies* 6 (Leiden: Brill, 1966), pp. 27-37.

[4] Henry J. Cadbury, *The Making of Luke-Acts* (London: S.P.C.K., 1927), "Factors in Composition," pp. 12-17. Cited in O. Lamar Cope, *Matthew: A Scribe Trained for the Kingdom of Heaven*, Catholic Biblical Quarterly Monograph Series 5 (Washington, D.C.: Catholic Biblical Association of America, 1976), p. 4.

[5] E. Lohmeyer, *Das Evangelium des Markus* (Meyer, 17th ed.; Göttingen: Vandenhoech und Ruprecht, 1967).

[6] R. H. Lightfoot, *History and Interpretation in the Gospels* (New York: Harper & Brothers, 1934); *Locality and Doctrine in the Gospels* (ibid., 1938).

[7] Hans Conzelmann, *Die Mitte der Zeit* (Tübingen: J. C. B. Mohr [Siebeck], 1953); Willi Marxsen, *Der Evangelist Markus* (Göttingen: Vandenhoeck und Ruprecht, 1956); Wolfgang Trilling, *Das wahre Israel*, Erfurter theologische Studien 7 (2d ed.; Leipzig: St. Benno Verlag, 1959); G. Bornkamm, G. Barth, and H.-J. Held, *Auslegung und Unterlieferung im Mätthausevangelium* (Neukirchen Verlag, 1960).

[8]John R. Donahue, *Are You the Christ?: The Trial Narrative in the Gospel of Mark*, Society of Biblical Literature Dissertation Series 10 (S.B.L.: Missoula, 1973).

[9]Gerhard Schneider, *Verleugnung, Verspottung und Verhör Jesu nach Lukas 22, 54-71* (München: Kösel-Verlag, 1969).

[10]Johannes Schreiber, *Die Theologie des Vertrauens: Eine redaktionsgeschichtliche Untersuchung des Markusevangeliums* (Hamburg: Furche Verlag, 1967); *Die Markuspassion: Wege zur Forschung der Leidensgeschichte Jesu* (ibid., 1969).

[11]Eta Linnemann, *Studien zur Passionsgeschichte*, FRLANT 102 (Göttingen: Vandenhoeck und Ruprecht, 1970).

[12]Gerhard Schneider, *Die Passion Jesu nach den drei älteren Evangelien* (München: Kösel-Verlag, 1973).

[13]*Jesus on Trial*, p. 38, n. 4, citing V. Taylor, *The Gospel According to St. Mark* (London: Macmillan, 1955), pp. 653-64. Cf. J. Jeremias, *The Eucharistic Words of Jesus*, tr. N. Perrin. (3d ed. rev.; New York: Scribner's, 1966), pp. 89-96, who distinguishes between a traditional short account beginning with the arrest and a long account.

[14]*Jesus on Trial*, p. 43, n. 11.

[15]Cf. Georg Braumann, "Markus 15, 2-5 und Markus 14, 55-64," *Zeitschrift für die neutestamentliche Wissenschaft* 52 (1961), pp. 273-78. S. G. F. Brandon holds the same view, *The Trial of Jesus of Nazareth* (New York: Stein & Day, 1968), pp. 105.

[16]Cf. *Jesus on Trial*, pp. 90-109, for a distinction between Luke's use of Markan pericopes in the hearings before the high priest and Pilate, and his reliance on his own material, e.g., the appearance of Jesus before Herod, 23:6-16.

[17]"There are a number of places where only Mark and John are in verbal agreement: the anointment of pure nard (Mark 14:3; John 12:3); the 300 denarii (Mark 14:5; John 12:5); Peter warming (*thermainomenos*) himself (Mark 14:54, 67; John 18:18, 25); Peter's going "into" the courtyard (Mark 14:54; John 18:15); the cry "crucify him" in the imperative (Mark 15:14, John 19:15); the purple robe (Mark 15:17; John 19:2, 5); the mention of the preparation day (Mark 15:42; John 19:31)." John R. Donahue, "Introduction: From Passion Traditions to Passion Narrative," in Werner H. Kelber, *The Passion in Mark: Studies on Mark 14-16* (Philadelphia: Fortress Press, 1976), p. 9. Donahue cites at this point X. Léon-Dufour, "Passion [Récits de la]," *Dictionnaire de la Bible, Supplément VI*, 1421-24.

[18]Norman Perrin, *What Is Redaction Criticism?* (Philadelphia: Fortress Press, 1969), p. 1.

[19]O. L. Cope, *op. cit.*, p. 3.

[20]Ibid.

[21]Ibid., p. 4, making use of Cadbury, *op. cit.*

[22]Donahue, *Are You the Christ?* p. 233.

[23]Ibid., pp. 222 f.

[24]Ibid., p. 58.

[25]Ibid., pp. 99 f.

[26]Ibid., p. 101.

[27]Ibid., p. 77.

[28]Ibid., p. 105; F. Hahn is cited for a survey of the opinions, *Mission in the New Testament*, Studies in Biblical Theology 47 (London: S.C.M. Press, 1965), p. 37, n. 1.

[29]Ibid., p. 106, n. 1.

[30]Ibid., p. 113; the analysis of the texts is given on pp. 113-35.

[31]Weeden (in Kelber, *The Passion in Mark*, "The Cross as Power in Weakness") thinks the statement false because it (and that in 15:29) attributes to Jesus a divine man christology and eschatology which Mark rejects, p. 125. Donahue holds the content true for Mark but grants that the form is false because it is uttered by Jesus, according to Mark, at the wrong time, i.e., before his enthronement and coming (ibid., "Temple, Trial," p. 67, n. 18).

[32]Donahue, *Are You the Christ?* p. 149.

[33]Ibid., p. 175.

[34]Ibid., pp. 176 f.

[35]*Jewish War*, 2.13, 6-7 #264-70; 2.18, 1-2 #457-65; 2.18, 5 #477-80; 2.18, 7-9 #487-506.

[36]*Jewish War*, 6.5, #300-09, in 6.5, 4 #312-13 an "ambiguous oracle" that one from the country of the Jews would be ruler of the world is named as the chief thing that led to resistance to Rome.

[37]Paul Winter, *On the Trial of Jesus* (2d ed. rev. and ed. T. A. Burkill and Geza Vermes; Berlin, N.Y.: Walter de Gruyter, 1974), p. 159.

[38]Donahue, *op. cit.*, p. 230.

[39]Max Wilcox, "The Denial Sequence in Mark XIV 26-31, 66-72," *New Testament Studies* 17 (July 1971), pp. 426-36, esp. pp. 433-36.

[40](Philadelphia: Fortress Press, 1976). Besides the contributors named above, there are essays by V. K. Robbins (14:12-25), W. H. Kelber (14:32-42), K. E. Dewey (14:53-54, 66-72), T. J. Weeden, Sr. (15:20b-41) and J. D. Crossan (16:1-8). The editor provides a conclusion entitled "From Passion Narrative to Gospel."

[41](Philadelphia: Westminster, 1961).

[42]Donahue notes that none of these authors cites Lindars, p. 3, no. 8.

[43]Donahue, "Temple, Trial, and Royal Christology" in Kelber, *op. cit.*, p. 63; cf. p. 65. For Braumann, cf. n. 15 above.

[44]Perrin, "The High Priest's Question" in ibid., p. 94.

[45]Kelber, "Conclusion" in ibid., p. 174. G. Bertram, as early as half a century ago, had thought Pilate's "wonder" the religious awe of the believer as part of a cult legend. Cf. *Die Leidensgeschichte Jesu und der Christoskult*, FRLANT NF 22(Göttingen: Vandenhoech und Ruprecht, 1922), pp. 5 f.

[46]Donahue, "Introduction," p. 14.

[47]Frans Neirynck, *Duality in Mark: Contributions to the Study of Markan Redaction*,Bibliotheca Ephemeridum Theologicarum Lovaniensium 31 (Leuven: Leuven University Press, 1972).

[48]Cf. Werner H. Kelber, *The Kingdom in Mark: A New Place and a New Time* (Philadelphia: Fortress Press, 1974); Theodore J. Weeden, *Mark: Traditions in Conflict* (ibid., 1971); Norman Perrin, "Towards an Interpretation of the Gospel of Mark" in *Christology and a Modern Pilgrimage,* ed. H. D. Betz (Claremont: New Testament Colloquium, 1971), pp. 1-78; ibid., *A Modern Pilgrimage in New Testament Christology* (Philadelphia: Fortress Press, 1974).

[49]Donahue, "Temple, Trial," p. 69.

[50]Ibid., pp. 74 f.; cf. Josephus *Antiquities* 8, #46-47.

[51]Cf. 1 Sam 21:1-6.

[52]D. H. Juel, *Message and Temple: The Trial of Jesus in the Gospel of Mark*, SBL Dissertation Series 31 (Missoula: Scholars Press, 1977).

[53]Lothar Ruppert, *Jesus als der leidende Gerechte?: Der Weg Jesu im Lichte eines alt- und zwischentestamentlichen Motivs*, Stuttgarter Bibelstudien 59 (Stuttgart: KBW Verlag, 1972).

[54]Ibid., *Der Leidende Gerechte: Eine motivgeschichtliche Untersuchung zum Alten Testament und zwischentestamentlichen Judentum*, Forschung zur Bibel 5 und 6 (Würzburg: Echter Verlag, 1972-73).

[55]Ruppert, *Jesus*, pp. 74 f.

[56]Ludger Schenke, *Studien zur Passionsgeschichte des Markus: Tradition und Redaktion in Markus 14, 1-42.* Forschung zur Bible 4 (Würzburg: Echter Verlag, 1971). The pre-Markan tradition includes: 14:3b-8, 12a, 13-16, 21b, 22b-24, 32, 33b, 34, 35a, 36-37, 38b, 40b, 42. Markan redaction is everything else up to vs. 41. This information is not available in any one place but is found scattered throughout the book.

[57]Ibid., *Der gekreuzigte Christus*, Stuttgarter Biblestudien 69 (Stuttgart: KBW, 1974), pp. 44-46, 60-62, 135-36.

[58]Johannes Schreiber, *Die Markuspassion: Wege zur Erforschung der Leidensgeschichte Jesu* (Hamburg: Furche-Verlag, 1969).

[59]Ibid., pp. 18-19, 27, 53. Kelber in *The Passion in Mark* cites seven verbal similarities of John to Mark in the Gethsemane pericope, Mark 14:35-42, p. 56, n. 35.

[60]Ibid., *Die Theologie des Vertrauens: Eine redaktionsgeschichtliche Untersuchung des Markusevangeliums* Hamburg: Furche-Verlag, 1967).

[61]Wolfgang Schenk, *Der Passionsbericht nach Markus* Gütersloh: Gerd Mohn, 1974).

[62]Detlev Dormeyer, *Die Passion Jesu als Verhaltensmodell: Literarische und theologische Analyse der Traditions-und Redaktionsgeschichte der Markuspassion* (Münster: Verlag Aschendorff, 1974).

[63]Cf. pp. 297-301 for the keyed Greek text.

[64]Ibid., p. 263.

[65]Ibid., pp. 277-79.

[66]Georg Strecker, *Der Weg der Gerechtigkeit: Untersuchung der Theologie des Mätthaus*, FRLANT 82 (Göttingen: Vandenhoeck und Ruprecht, 1962; 2d rev. ed. 1966).

[67]Wolfgang Trilling, *Das wahre Israel: Studien zum Theologie des Matthaüsevangeliums*, Erfurter Theologische Studien 7 (Leipzig: St. Benno, 1959; 3d rev. ed., Studien xum Alten und Neuen Testament 10, München: 1964).

[68]Donald P. Senior, *The Passion Narrative According to Matthew: A Redactional Study*, Bibliotheca Ephemeridum Theologicarum Lovaniensium 39 (Leuven: Leuven University Press, 1975). It was preceded by the same author's "The Passion Narrative in the Gospel of Matthew," in *L' évangile selon Matthieu*, ed. M. Didier, Bibliotheca Ephemeridum Theologicarum Lovaniensium 29 (Gembloux: Duculot, 1972), pp. 343-57; cf. A. Descamps. "Rédaction et christologie dans le récit matthéen de la Passion," ibid., pp. 359-415.

[69]Senior, *Passion Narrative*, p. 335.

[70]Ibid.

[71]Ibid., p. 336.

[72]Ibid., p. 181.

[73]David Catchpole, "The Answer of Jesus to Caiaphas (Matt. xxvi. 64), *New Testament Studies* 17 (1971), pp. 213-26.

[74]Senior, p. 261.

[75]Ibid., p. 338.

[76]David Catchpole, *The Trial of Jesus: A Study in the Gospels and Jewish Historiography from 1770 to the*

Present Day (Leiden: Brill, 1971), pp. 183 ff.

[77]Vincent Taylor, *The Passion Narrative of St. Luke*, SNTS Monograph Series 19 (Cambridge: University Press, 1972).

[78]Ibid., pp. 272-78

[79]Schneider, *Verleugnung*, p. 134.

[80]Ibid., p. 166, n. 6.

[81]Ibid., pp. 61-70.

[82]Anton Dauer, *Die Passionsgeschichte im Johannesevangelium: Eine traditionsgeschichtliche und theologische Untersuchung zu Joh 18, 1-19, 30* (München: Kösel-Verlag, 1972).

[83]Ibid., p. 286.

[84]See also F. Hahn, *Der Prozess Jesu nach dem Johannesevangelium*, in EKK 2 (Zürich-Einsiedeln-Köln-Neukirchen), 1970.

[85]Ernst Haenchen, "History and Interpretation in the Johannine Passion Narrative," *Interpretation* 24 (1970), 198-219; tr. by James P. Martin from an essay of the same title in *Zur Bedeutung des Todes Jesu*, ed. Fritz Viering (Gütersloh: Gerd Mohn, 1967), pp. 57-78.

[86]Hans Conzelmann, "History and Theology in the Passion Narratives of the Synoptic Gospels," ibid., p. 190, n. 21; tr. by C. B. Cousar, pp. 37-53.

[87]Ernest Best, *The Temptation and the Passion* (Cambridge: University Press, 1965).

[88]Ernst Haenchen, *Der Weg Jesu* Berlin: Verlag Alfred Topelmann, 1966).

HISTORY AND FAITH:

PAST AND FUTURE

THE HISTORICAL JESUS:
Two Views of His Significance for Twentieth-Century Christianity

Paul Misner

Beyond Stereotypes

Among the Christian religious thinkers of the early part of this century few are more fascinating than the Liberal Protestant, Nathan Söderblom, and the Catholic Modernist, George Tyrrell. A resurgence of interest in both of them is taking place at present,[1] perhaps because neither can easily be confined within the usual stereotypes of Liberal Protestantism and Modernism. Tyrrell was a restless, intense personality, whose writing shows signs of the struggle between a mind prone to skepticism and a religious, indeed "incurably Christocentric," soul. His thought lies like a tangled skein of threads, some worn thin, others broken or lying across each other in apparent contradiction in his books, articles and letters. It is difficult to tell which ones actually are twisted together in mutual reinforcement, like the wires in a cable. The interpreter of Söderblom faces a similar problem, but not to the same degree. Söderblom had unshaken convictions to express. He radiated the utmost confidence both in his rather prolix writings and in his prototypical activism as a mover and shaker of ecclesiastical inertia in his campaign for cooperation of the churches in "Life and Work."

Theologically the two had a great deal in common.
Both were sure that religion in the last analysis was
something other and higher than the spiritual life engendered by immanent forces in humankind. Both had personally experienced and realized the shortcomings of
intellectualist theology, Tyrrell in the form of neo-
Scholasticism and Söderblom in the Protestant insistence
on the inerrancy of the Bible. Thus both understood
religious language, including doctrinal formulations,
as symbolic. Söderblom had the good fortune of finding
leading representatives of Protestant theology (Schleier-
macher and Ritschl along with Auguste Sabatier) who made
brilliant use of this principle. Tyrrell felt constrained to develop an approach peculiar to himself by
positing a wordless and changeless revelation and contrasting with it theology as coherent discourse always
subject to change. In between was the realm of prophetic and other frankly symbolic discourse and expression (in words, but also in events and persons). It was
theology's task to try to translate the symbols in intel-
lectually satisfying form: the attempt was indispensable,
but complete success was out of the question. Those
who thought that theology could communicate revelation
in an unmetaphorical way were victims of "theologism,"
an ideology rampant among scholastics who had never
taken the phrase, *docta ignorantia,* to heart.

Two other leading themes sharing an uneasy cohabi-
tation in Tyrrell's thought were catholicity and conscience, to both of which Söderblom could respond
sympathetically. Tyrrell saw Christianity at a cross-
roads, facing an "impasse." There was no going back
to any earlier synthesis of faith and culture; a new one

was desperately needed. He was convinced that Catholicism provided the broadest and best religious raw material for a future synthesis and that Protestantism had too narrow a basis to serve in that capacity. In his *Christianity at the Cross-Roads* he pronounced what later became a common judgment on the cultural Protestantism of the nineteenth century, that it was bankrupt. Söderblom never could accept this judgment, being himself living proof that a Liberal Protestant could have catholic sympathies in things religious and believe passionately in the Christ of the Christian tradition. Later he coined the term, "Evangelic Catholicity," for the attitude he would try to promote in the various Christian churches. That Ritschl, Herrmann and Harnack would be superseded, he knew very well; that one could consider them irreligious, however, bespoke a regrettable lapse in objectivity and fairmindedness.

One recent study of Tyrrell's philosophy of religion (Faupel, pp. 258-77) suggests that the central religious phenomenon around which all of his thinking revolved was conscience. Tyrrell therefore expressed the normativeness of Christ by linking him substantially with the universal human mystery of conscience (Tyrrell 1909, p. 177). If Söderblom could have perceived this link-up more clearly, it certainly would have appealed to him, but he was thrown off by Tyrrell's insistence that morality was subordinate to religion and remained essentially an innerworldly concern, whereas religion had to do with the transcendent. Not so for Söderblom: to him the heart of the Gospel came to light in the conscience stricken with a sense of sin and liberated by grace to a generous life of service, which he considered an event

of the moral order. One can recognize here the influence
of the Lutheran emphasis on the doctrine of justification
by faith as the summary of the Gospel (1910a, pp. 337-51
with p. 503; Söderblom to Heiler, 4 August 1926, in
Misner, ed.).

Other parallels could be noted, but before we go
on to examine the respective pastoral situations and aims
of the two men, a basic difference should be mentioned.
This is the dominant influence exercised in Söderblom's
thinking by the conviction that God works through history.
The foremost instance of this was of course the salvation
wrought by God through Jesus Christ, but in a way that
was probably unique for his time Söderblom did not limit
the application to Christ or biblical history (Sharpe,
p. 159). It functioned as the basic inspiration of his
work in the history of religions as well as a criterion
of the adequacy of any Christian theology to the religious
problems of the modern world. Though incomprehensible to
historicists, this theological principle enabled Söderblom
to transcend their dilemma (absoluteness of Christianity
versus relative validity of any religion) by a simultaneous
affirmation of God's unique self-revelation in Christ and
of the authentic relationship to the absolute or to the
higher world found also in other religions. Philosophic-
ally it was consonant with the interpretation of existence
as life (which he espoused and attributed also to Bergson);
theologically it afforded a reinterpretation of the doctrine
of a general revelation; as a philosophy of history it
owed much to Grundtvig and Hjärne (Söderblom 1933, pp.
371-75); and the historian or religions could argue for
it on purely historical-phenomenological grounds (ibid.,
p. xxviii).

Presumably one of the reasons why Söderblom decided
to teach a major course on Modernism and turn the lecture
notes into a big book was the Modernists' own emphasis
on history. In the end, however, he found their historical consciousness still underdeveloped. As long as they
remained Modernists (and it was to Tyrrell's credit that
he remained one to the end), their attachment to Catholicism was too strong for them to carry through consistently
the idea of a revelation in history without making the
church its exclusive medium. What that meant in the concrete will become apparent as we compare Söderblom and
Tyrrell on Jesus' preaching of the Kingdom of God.

History as a Challenge to the Chruches: Tyrrell

George Tyrrell (1861-1909) belonged to the Church
of Ireland until he was received into the Roman Catholic
communion in 1879. He entered the Jesuits almost simultaneously and became a much-read author of essays on
spiritual and theological topics in England. Like many
contemporaries he became more and more convinced of the
futility and irrelevance of traditional apologetics, and
he welcomed the assistance received from his older friend,
Baron Friedrich von Hügel, in familiarizing himself with
all the new attempts that were being made by Catholic and
Protestant thinkers to frame a more adequate theological
response to the times. It was in the year 1902 that he
became aware of where the shoe was pinching most acutely.
It was then that he read *Jesus' Proclamation of the Kingdom of God* by Johannes Weiss (the Baron had insisted that
he learn to read German) and shortly thereafter *The Gospel
and the Church* by Loisy.[2] Independently of each other,

both exegetes had worked out a reading of the synoptic
Gospels (or rather their sources) which was startlingly
different from, and hence threatening to, the traditionally received beliefs of Christians.[3] As von Hügel recalled
in a letter to Söderblom on 13 April 1910, it had been a
"violent shock" to Tyrrell, "when he read for the first
time Johannes Weiss's *Die Predigt Jesu vom Reiche Gottes*
and seemed to have squarely before his eyes a Jesus who
believed naively" in such things as demonic possession;
or that such conceptions as the struggle going on between
the Rule of God and the Rule of Satan were not metaphorical
to Jesus, but the plain truth to be seen in his exorcisms
and in his ministry of forgiveness and soon to be brought
to a definitive climax with the establishment of a new
order of things through God's power.

A few months later Tyrrell read Loisy's book and
wrote his first letter to the eminent savant, noting
inter alia:

> What especially pleased me in *L'Evangile et l'Eglise*
> is the manner in which you have assimilated and
> rendered helpful, instead of harmful, the somewhat
> disconcerting position of Weiss's *Predigt Jesu vom
> Reiche Gottes*-- a book which had given me consider-
> able pause (20 Nov. 1902, in Petre 1912, II, 394).

Loisy made a strong case, as against Harnack, that the
eschatologically-minded Jesus of the sources was the logical impetus for the immense development of Christianity
that followed in the Catholic Church with its doctrine,
worship and organization. To take Jesus as a teacher of
sublime morality, but a morality for the present life (as
Harnack did after Ritschl), was not only a forced reading
of the texts about Jesus but also made it difficult to
account for the rise of Christianity. Tyrrell was not an
uncritical admirer of Loisy and felt that the appeal to

conscience as a life-shaping force might be the element
that Liberal Protestants such as Harnack or Matthew
Arnold should contribute to a synthesis (letter of Tyrrell
to Hügel of 4 December 1902 in Petre 1912, II, 396 and
1937, p. 115). His attitude hardened against Liberal
Protestantism, however, owing to the pressure of polemics
(von Hügel to Söderblom, 13 April 1910, in Misner, ed.).
In *Cross-Roads* (p. 76) Tyrrell regarded Loisy's approach
as sound and based his own arguments on it.

The church's great need at the beginning of the
twentieth century was, in Tyrrell's mind, to overcome
its backwardness in respect to the existing state of
reflective thought and science. The church had committed
itself so thoroughly to the paradigm of a bygone age,
through its overly rational but official theology, that
efforts to loosen up the calcified articulations of doctrine to permit some flexibility and movement and thereby
the possibility of dealing with new questions, met with
less and less success. Any endeavour to "baptize" elements of modern thinking systematically, as Thomas Aquinas
had once baptized Aristotelian thought, were even more
clearly doomed to failure by drowning. The soul-chilling
spectacle of the treatment meted out by the church's
leaders and shapers of opinion to those who were trying
loyally to mediate between tradition and modern thought
brought out the despairing, "apocalyptic" excess of these
prognistications. In calmer moments he granted: "Amid
all the protective theological accretions the nucleus of
Christianity has been preserved like a fly in amber, or
like a mommoth in ice; while outside theology, the spirit
of Christ has lived and developed in the life of the
faithful collectively" (Petre 1912, II, 218). In a letter

to von Hügel of 7 April 1909, reflecting his state of
mind while writing *Cross Roads*, he said: "Few of our
apparent allies have really grasped or believed in the
Modernist position. . . . They do not believe that modernity has anything to learn from the Church, but only
that the Church has everything to learn from modernity"
(Petre 1937, p. 202; cf. Söderblom 1910a, p. 219).

To whom was Tyrrell referring? To Buonaiuti primarily, and to the other Italian Modernists for whom the
Christ of eschatology was a direct warrant for socialism
(not that socialism as a political program was repugnant
to Tyrrell, but he regarded it as a poor religion). The
problems of Italian Modernism were instrumental in leading Tyrrell to focus even more on the figure of Jesus and
his strange-sounding eschatological message than on the
blatant present shortcomings of the church. The acid
test of the confrontation of Christianity and modernity
was the question of Jesus' Kingdom proclamation and its
bearing on Christian faith and living. Not only the
Italian situation, of course, but also the previous
inconclusive controversy over Loisy's book, indicated the
centrality of this question.[4] Historical understanding
represented to a preeminent degree the accomplishments of
the modern mind; the pastoral challenge was to recast
the teaching about Christ so that the critical attitude
of the scientist and historian would show the way to a
more solid grounding of the place occupied by Christ in
Christian faith and devotion. Whatever may be thought of
Tyrrell's handling of the subject, his intuition that
eschatology would be a critical question in the theology
of the subsequent period has been borne out to the fullest.
Theology is still feeling tremors from the quake that
Weiss and Loisy registered on their seismographs.

Söderblom and Historical Criticism

The role of historical criticism was not less crucial
to the life and thought of the later Archbishop Söderblom
(1866-1931, Archbishop of Uppsala from 1914). He had
grown up in the pietistic tradition of Swedish Lutheranism, represented for him by his own father, a pastor.
It was a painful process for him to come eventually to
a recognition of the legitimacy of historical criticism
in biblical studies and reconcile it with the lively
faith of his father, whom he esteemed and wished to emulate.
But when the process was finally endured, Nathan Söderblom
emerged with a solidity, confidence and activism of faith
which remains deeply impressive to the present day. All
this took place during his university years, while Tyrrell
was still relishing the discovery of Thomas Aquinas. The
theological master who paved the way for Söderblom was
Albrecht Rischl, with his strong appeal to the moral
values seen in the example of Jesus. Nevertheless the
historical-critical questions which seemed disturbing at
the time were not yet those of the historical Jesus (this
was still before Weiss's publication), but concerned the
authorship of the Pentateuch, the inerrancy of the scripture, and other problems thrown up principally by Old
Testament studies (Akerberg, p. 301, cf. p. 112). An
initial factor which helped Söderblom overcome his crisis
was the simple observation of a Ritschlian theologian that
the Bible is composed largely of occasional pieces, not
written in the first instance to provide a theological
system and certainly not to be applied *directly* and
uncritically to the solution of modern problems.

I have not been able to determine just when Söderblom came across Weiss's description of the eschatological

framework of Jesus' preaching of the Kingdom of God, or whether it gave him pause (as Tyrrell put it). But presumably it was in the 1890s, as Söderblom was preparing his doctoral dissertation on the eschatology of Iranian Mazdéisme for the Protestant Theology Faculty of the Sorbonne (published 1901). During that period he familiarized himself with the work of Gunkel and Bousset of the "history of religions school" of Old Testament studies as well as with R. H. Charles's edition and studies of apocalyptic works. In any case, it is clear that Söderblom was among those Liberal Protestant scholars who accepted Weiss's reading of the synoptic gospels. More than most others, it seems, he succeeded in integrating this historical picture in his rather open theological construction, with the aid of a philosophy of action of Parisian provenance.

Since the theology of Liberal Protestantism in its German and French forms had been such a help to his own life of faith, Söderblom was inclined to think that the further progress of Christian thought in the modern age would be along lines not inconsistent with Ritschl's work. This he did not regard as a closed scholastic system, but as a modern historical approach capable of indefinite modification as the ongoing context of science and culture might demand. This is why he accepted the *Jesusbild* of Weiss and had only reservations of detail concerning the interpretations of Loisy and Schweitzer. These corrected certain unhistorical assumptions of other modern interpreters, but corroborated the need affirmed, for example, by A. Sabatier, that traditional expressions of faith (those of the Bible included) must be taken as

symbols. That this could lead to reducing Jesus' whole
significance to the immanent, or even the purely psychological, plane, was a danger in a positivistic age, to
be sure. But it does not seem to have been a live option
for Söderblom himself, now that he had emerged from his
earlier crisis. In short, he does not seem to have shared
the perspective of most other observers, who insist on
the fundamental and irreconcilable differences between
Ritschl's construction and the historical-critical findings of his son-in-law, Weiss.[5]

If we ask how Söderblom viewed the situation and
the challenge of Christianity in the twentieth century,
two factors are foremost. As a historian of religions,
he was acutely conscious of what we now call "planetiza-
tion" and he expected the inherent rivalry between Buddhism and Christianity to become more and more pronounced.
To him, each of these world religions constituted a religious ultimate in its own way.[6] The fact of Buddhism and
of the oriental religions in general constituted an important point of reference for Söderblom in the consideration of the historical Jesus. Buddha also figures prom-
inently in Tyrrell's reflections on the subject, but without Söderblom's magisterial comparative-religions overview (see below). What Christianity needed most, and most
painfully lacked in Söderblom's perspective, became clear
after he became Archbishop of Uppsala. It was a common
witness and a coordinated service to a divided world.
The situation of division, suspicion and rancor among
Christian bodies was what had to be overcome most of all.
With a world-spanning activism he strove for the kind
of Christian unity which would give testimony to their
common faith in Christ through a common engagement in the

practical realm of peace and justice. As the organizer
of the movement for Life and Work (and of its first inter-
national conference of Churches in Stockholm, 1925) he
was one of the founders of the ecumenical movement which
is now embodied especially in the World Council of Churches.
He used to put his thinking on Christian ecumenism into
a nutshell by saying that the Roman Church had built up
an institutional unity which was unique in Christendom
and had been a worthy realization of Christian unity as
far as it went--but was no longer a serviceable model.
Luther had vindicated a more essential touchstone of Christian unity, right faith in salvation through Christ alone--
but this was in practice a divisive factor. Yet there is
a still more excellent way. Without surrender of any
Christian's most deeply-held convictions, all should
follow the commandment of love in service of their neigh-
bors. In a world rapidly becoming one, the hour has come
for the churches to break out of their isolation and
follow this way of love tegether.

The Historical Jesus and His Message to the Churches: Tyrrell

Tyrrell's *Cross-Roads* abounds in paradoxes. The
chief paradox lies perhaps in the very intentions of the
author. He had been barred from the sacraments since 1905
and excommunicated since 1907, after he had publicly
attacked the papal encyclical condemning Modernism,
Pascendi. Then he wrote a searing indictment of *Medieval-
ism* (1908). When he died after a short illness, it was
hardly expected that his last book would be a defense of
Catholic tradition (needless to say in a new mode), of

the sacraments, beliefs and practices of the Catholic
Church. He did this by working out the implications, as
he saw them, of the historical Jesus recently brought to
light by Weiss and Loisy and by contrasting them with a
polemically simplified version of Liberal Protestantism.
In his hands one last overriding paradox took shape and
dominated his argument: the Jesus of the eschatological
interpretation of the most liberal (= critical) scholars
was an affront to modernity!

The Jesus that Tyrrell presented to his readers was
a prophet and more than a prophet. He proclaimed the
imminent coming of God's Rule in human society and, in
contrast to John the Baptist, acted as its designated
Messiah. With John, Elijah had already come; the out-
pouring of the Spirit before the End was at hand; the
tribulation preceding God's victory also loomed--thus the
apocalyptic stage was set. Though Jesus was reserved
in speaking of himself--it was a matter which would be
revealed for all to see soon enough in any case--it is
possible that he looked upon himself in his earthly condition as the Son of David, who would come on the clouds
as the heavenly Son of Man with the onset of the Kingdom
(pp. 50-52, 56-57, 69-70, 123). In Jesus' setting this
might have been conceived along the lines of "possession,"
as a divinely effected parallel to the action of demonic
spirits in "possessing" human beings (pp. 54, 172). All
this is quite questionable, to say the least, from the
perspective of today's research, but equivalently high
claims on Jesus' part are still seen to be implicit in
his words and actions. We will later cite another example
of a point (taken from Schweitzer) that has not stood the
test of time.

More important is Tyrrell's notion of the relationship between the world-view of the prophets in the Old
Testament and apocalypticism. He knew that "the apocalyptic literature was an exotic, a late introduction
into the religion of Israel" (p. 81). Nevertheless he
regarded Jesus' eschatology as identical with "that of the
Jewish apocalyptics, with the difference that He Himself
was destined to be the Son of Man" (p. 50). Had not the
prophets looked forward to a consummation of God's purpose
within the ongoing conditions of earthly life? "The
decay of that prophetic hope had introduced the more radical apocalyptic hope. The Kingdom of God was not to be
realized by any gradual development of the present order,
but by an irruption of the supernatural order" (p. 51,
cf. p. 91). Thus also Jesus' quality of being the Son of
David was subordinated to the apocalyptic figure of the
coming Son of Man, as Tyrrell conjectured.

Of course, the main similarity between Jesus' vision
and apocalypticism was for Tyrrell the conviction that
the present world order only had a short existence left,
since God would vindicate the hopes of his faithful ones
within the generation to which Jesus delivered his message. This immediacy was the expression of the urgency
with which one must respond to the Good News. It was
announced as a present and pressing invitation which
allowed of no indecision, no matter how long the clock
of the age would continue to tick. Jesus could not be
aware of all that he symbolized. The Christian will thus
be anxious to alleviate the earth's misery, to take one
example, by virtue of the hopes wakened in him or her by
Jesus' preaching, even though Jesus himself depended on
the timely coming of the new order to put an end to it
(p. 118).

What Jesus looked forward to, after all, was "the
speedy advent of a new world, a world in which ethics
would be superseded" (p. 52). The time-table was not
important--Jesus simply assumed it or conjectured it on
the basis of the vivid presentments which he had of the
Kingdom (p. 62)--but the plan of God subsumed under the
idea of the Kingdom was incontestably of a transcendental
order.

> Men were to be transformed and glorified: heaven
> and earth were to be transfigured; the just were to
> eat the same spiritual meat and drink the same
> spiritual drink at the heavenly banquet with Abraham,
> Isaac and Jacob; there was to be no more death
> or sorrow or sin or temptation, for the former
> things were to pass away. The poor, the meek, the
> peacemakers, the merciful, the pure, the mourners,
> the hungerers after justice, the persecuted would
> be so no more (p. 52).

Moreover, Jesus could no more regard his portrayal of
this other-worldly consummation as symbolic or as culturally conditioned than he could have discoursed learnedly
on Hegelian dialectics (cf. p. 81). "For Jesus, what we
call His apocalyptic 'imagery' was no mere imagery but
literal fact" (p. 77). Even though *we* must understand
that his preaching was couched in symbolic forms, this
does not mean that we must reduce his message from the
transcendental to the historical level.

This at least was Tyrrell's conviction and the
basis of his complaint against Harnack and the Liberal
Protestant portrayal of Jesus in general. The latter
supposed that Jesus' quarrel was with a set of ethonocen-
tric expectations nurtured by his fellow Jews and that
he countered this with a moral disinterestedness, an
inward Rule of God in the souls of the upright. But even
Weiss had recognized that this would not stand up

historically. "Jesus did not oppose a moral to a worldly
interpretation of the Kingdom. He took the current interpretation as He found it, which was not worldly but other-
worldly--spiritual, in the sense of metaphysical and transcendent, not in the immanental moral sense" (*Cross-Roads*,
p. 57). Over many subsequent pages Tyrrell then drew
out the analogies between the religion of Catholics, which
had retained this transcendent or supernatural understanding of the Gospel and of the original apocalyptic symbol-
ism in which Jesus had communicated it. For the Catholic
form of Christianity had preserved "the earthen vessel"
of expressive symbols "with its heavenly treasure,"
while "those who have broken and cast away the vessel
seem to have lost much of the treasure. Ought we not
still to keep it while carefully distinguishing it from
its content?" (p. 145).

Söderblom on Jesus' Eschatology

As he wrote to Baron von Hügel on 1 March 1910,
Söderblom had taken *Cross-Roads* into his hands with a
great sense of anticipation, perhaps even expecting too
much (cf. Söderblom 1910a, p. 209). He welcomed the
portrayal of the eschatological Christ which dominated the
book as an important contribution to dissemination of
knowledge outside of specialist circles, but he was
disappointed by the confessionalistic tone in which
Tyrrell chose to deliver his polemics. There were already
more than enough emotionally skewed half-truths hindering
the theological exchange between Christian Churches; he
did not expect Tyrrell, of all people, to add to them.
Söderblom was also of the opinion that Tyrrell did

not quite grasp the exact bearing of the exegetical discussion concerning the eschatology of Jesus. All the same,
on the sticking point for the vast majority of Christian
believers, the contention that Jesus really expected the
end of this world order and the establishment of a new
one by God in the immediate future, Söderblom both con-
curred with the exegetical findings as Tyrrell presented
them and offered a strikingly similar interpretation for
pastoral purposes. The expectation of the Kingdom in
the near future lent Jesus' message a remarkable force,
earnestness and urgency, which alone could do justice to
the otherworldly quality and reality of which he was the
revealer (1910b, pp. 280 and 199; cf. 1910a, pp. 215-16
and 1933, 369-70). He also welcomed the fundamental option
defended by Tyrrell, which he paraphrased in this way:
"On one of the two roads which Christianity can take into
the future, religion is an infinitely important and pre-
cious, but innerworldly, evolution, belonging to the historical and cultural process; on the other road one
catches echoes of strange noises from a heavenly world,
and the human soul itself grows wings" (1910a, p. 217).
The Jesus who emerges from critical analysis of the texts
certainly stands for the second way.

However, Tyrrell's conception of the difference
between prophetic and apocalyptic hopes was misleading.
The prophet was rightly characterized as "driven by the
Spirit" (Tyrrell 1909, p. 171; cf. Söderblom 1910a, p.
213), but for what purpose? To work out a complicated
report of a heavenly vision according to an esoteric pattern, where each element in the vision corresponded to
and predetermined events on earth? That is the procedure
of the apocalyptic writers. But the prophets simply

proclaimed the word of the Lord unto judgment or promise, without any of the highly involved scenery of arcane apocalyptic lore. If Tyrrell would just compare the book of Jeremiah with the book of Enoch, for instance, he would see at once where Jesus' affinities lie. Even if the synoptic "apocalypse" should go back to Jesus' own preaching, it would still be clear that he stands in the authentic prophetic tradition and declines to follow apocalyptic precedents.

It also seemed rather far-fetched to Söderblom to limit the moral life to our dealings with and in the present order, if that was really Tyrrell's intention, and hence to place the prophets as spokesmen of morality and conscience on a lower level than apocalyptic as a portrayal of spiritual religion ("Mysticism," Tyrrell, p. 171). Tyrrell himself could not avoid admitting that "Jesus' whole emphasis was on the other world and"--here follows what Söderblom sees as peculiarly characteristic of Jesus in contrast to other examples of Jewish apocalyptic--"on the conditions by which men might attain it and flee from the wrath to come. Of these, repentance and true inward righteousness were the chief" (Tyrrell, p. 61). The release of this kind of moral force was to Söderblom "*the* essential" specific of Jesus' preaching. The urgent mood of eschatological expectations corresponds to its importance. The curiosity to know when, where and how the Kingdom will come is typical of apocalypticism, but it surfaces in the Gospels only to be rebuffed. Not so with the appeal to conscience and faith, which Tyrrell tried to relegate to a subordinate place in Jesus' message (Söderblom 1910a, pp. 215-16, cf. Tyrrell, p. 119).

Tyrrell was no doubt lured into extremes by his opposition to the Liberal Protestant rejection of the supernatural and the metaphysical (not shared by Söderblom and hence not taken as essential to the Liberal Protestant position). Apparently some questionable traits in Schweitzer's "consistently eschatological" rendering of the historical Jesus (1906) confirmed him in his onesidedness. Schweitzer concluded among other things that it was a real source of consternation to Jesus that the Kingdom failed to come as he had predicted in Matt 10:23; thereupon Jesus decided to provoke the authorities to put him to death and thus, as Tyrrell put it, "hasten the issue" (pp. 55, 68). It is generally acknowledged now that this is going beyond what the sources can tell us. In Söderblom's view, it distorted the picture that *does* arise from the sources: Jesus' faith in the Kingdom was not shaken, because it was not concentrated so exclusively on a future event. The effect of his eschatological persuasions was emphatically not to devalue the present moment, but quite the opposite, to make the present time of decision all the more crucial because of its shortness (see 1910b). This approach is up to this point not very different from Tyrrell's and has been shared by many expositors since the turn of the century. It could be called an existential interpretation. But is it apocalyptic? A true or typical apocalyptic might have dropped everything on perceiving the nearness of the new age, in order to gaze intently at the stars and wrest from them the information that he wanted so avidly to possess. But Jesus invited his hearers to realize in their daily lives the moral qualities that were worthy of the Kingdom he and they anticipated. He reserved for himself the role of Son of Man and

this made him, it is true, more than a prophet. The
"more" in question, however, lay on the extension of the
authentically prophetic line, and had little to do with
the special characteristics of apocalypticism.

We will have to return to Söderblom's broader objec-
tions to Tyrrell's understanding of apocalyptic and prophecy in the next section; this applies also to the
phenomenon of "mysticism" and its place in the life of
Jesus. Ritschl, it is well known, waged a campaign
against mysticism of the pietistic variety because he
saw it as undermining faith in the evangelic sense.
Tyrrell, on the other hand, took Jesus to be in some sense
a "mystic and seer" (p. 50), his religion suggestive of
"the visionary or the ecstatic" (p. 123), although he
distinguishes "the mysticism of Jesus" from a thoroughgoing *fuga* or *contemptus mundi* (pp. 119, 171). The union
with God which is the goal of mysticism is, according to
Tyrrell, in the case of Jesus a conscious union with a
personal "Will that is at work in the whole process of
history and in every human soul" (ibid.). Overlooking
this last remark, Söderblom objected that Tyrrell was
generalizing his reaction against Liberal Protestant ideas
instead of keeping to the texts, "which . . . exclude the
desired type of a mystic" (1910a, p. 212). Söderblom
had a quite definite idea of what constitutes mysticism,
one drawn from comparative religion rather than theology.
There is a distinction that can be more fully appreciated
and more consistently applied than Tyrrell did between
a "mysticism of the infinite" and a "mysticism of personal
life: (p. 124). The failure to do so was the root of
what was unsatisfactory in Tyrrell's thought, as indeed
was also the case with von Hügel's writings on "the

mystical element of religion" (cf. the book of that title by von Hügel, 1908).

The Contribution of Comparative Religion

Christianity at the Cross-Roads contains a "Part II" (pp. 149-82), which is generally little noticed, headed "Christianity and Religion" (but cf. Ratté, p. 244). It discusses the issues of a universal religion, the absolute-ness of Christianity and the significance for Christianity of that novelty, the "Science of Religions." Curiously enough, not even Söderblom, the historian of religions, took any special notice of these last chapters and their relation to the rest of the book. All the same, the final chapter in Söderblom's book (pp. 443-71) seems to be almost a direct response to a suggestion of Tyrrell's about the role of a science of religions worthy of the name in the future of Christian thought (p. 165). The later wondered if it might not be possible with its aid to determine the laws of religion in general. He continued: "Should such a science, in the course of time, shape itself out of the present historical and pyschological study of exist-ing and bygone religions, it could not fail to exert a powerful influence on the various living embodiments of the religious idea; of which none could long survive which was known to defy the laws of its life" (ibid.). Now Söderblom was diffident about the prospects of deter-mining "the laws of religion in general," especially in the evolutionary perspective suggested by Tyrrell. But he did have a typology from the comparative study of religions which he felt it was important for theology to examine, especially in view of the strained relations

Between modernity and Christianity which were evident on
all sides. Without developing a clear front against
historicism, he did recognize that contemporary Protestant
thought was no more immune to it than Catholic Modernism
(1910a, pp. 441-43).

What Tyrrell made of the hypotheses then current
in history of religions boiled down to a three-stage
schema of its development on evolutionary lines: first
a magical stage, then a moral one (where he located the
prophets as teachers of an ethics superior to self-inter-
est), and finally a spiritual stage. Here that which is
irreducible about religion, the God who "reveals himself
as a mysterious, transcendent force . . . through the
action of spiritual personalities" comes into its own
(Tyrrell, pp. 170, 96, 168). What is properly religious
about the lower and middle stages of religion was their
sense of being ways for human beings to adjust themselves
to an unseen world (pp. 59, 79: this was Tyrrell's
"practical definition" of religion). But the forces
which magic tried to control have been demystified; innerworldly ethical concerns can be dealt with rationally as
well, leaving the concerns of spiritual religion to be
appreciated as otherworldly.

For his part Söderblom placed the emphasis on the
comparison of different *types* rather than different stages
of religion. Such types can be distinguished especially
at what Tyrrell would consider the higher stages. Thus
the sacred writings of both Israel and India testify to
a higher reality than that which meets the eye, but their
ways of talking about it differs and leads one to suspect
a typically different experience of the transcendent in
each tradition (pp. 461-71). One can in fact take a

bird's-eye view of the major religious developments in the history of the race and formulate some initial conclusions on that basis. On the one hand there is a religious sensibility concerned with the riddle of the world of nature and culture in relationship to spirit. An ascetical and mystical spirituality seems to develop almost inevitably, given a certain level of civilization and reflection, as happened both in ancient India and in Greece, where the tension of world (or matter) and spirit is felt. Its finest fruit and highest development is a "mysticism of infinity," theistic or non-theistic as the case may be, but consistently characterized by a longing for perfect union of the incorporeal self with the One and All, a union which tends toward annihilation of the self. Plotinus can stand as a model of this type. Hinduism and Buddhism continue to provide vigorous exemplifications of it in the present.

The other main type in the history of religions may be called "prophetical religion," since it originated in the experiences and influence of prophetic figures of Israel (Moses, the prophets known as such, Jesus, Paul and a succession of other outstanding individuals down to the present time) and also of Iran (Zarathustra) and Arabia (Mohammed). It does not necessarily presuppose the same level of material and intellectual culture as the emergence of mystical religion does, and it is a quite independent development, not necessarily issuing in an infinity-oriented mysticism as its ultimate consequence. It is also called "religion of revelation" in the special sense that the higher reality in the face of which it assumes its contours is experienced as a person acting in history (cf. Söderblom 1903, pp. 32-57 and 1944, pp. 308-15). Monotheism is congenital to this type of religion, because the God to whom the prophets harken will have none other beside him, but demands total loyalty. The relationship of mutual trust between a revealing God and his faithful leads to characteristic beliefs in the good outcome of the human story (eschatology). As an internalized religious faith of individuals it can lead to developments which can be called mystical in a broad sense, but with a difference. The communion with God which is here attained is personal, relational, dynamic, history-oriented (1903, pp. 68-73), in all of which the contrast with the mysticism of the Indian or Hellenic cast is evident. "Personality-affirming mysticism" (1910a, pp. 258-63) may be mixed with infinity mysticism in the life of the soul and especially in the attempts to describe and systematize intense religious experience, but as an ideal type it is quite distinctive.

This typology showed its fruitfulness especially in the classic work of Friedrich Heiler, *Prayer* (1918).[7] Here one can also see its application to the Protestant-Catholic difference in the Western Chruch. In a simplified form one could say that both Söderblom and Heiler regarded the Catholic ideal as basically infinity-oriented, though also taking up impulses from the prophetical tradition, whereas Protestant piety stresses the biblical heritage affirmative of personality and history.

How far Söderblom kept to the phenomenological-historical terrain in all this and refrained from implying value judgments is debatable (cf. Söderblom 1933, p. 317). He himself separated the value he acknowledged for himself theologically in Christian revelation from the phenomenological distinction of types. But he offered his contributions out of comparative religions to the theologians in

the hope that it would help them clarify the differences
between Christianity and other prevailing forms of religion without denying the religious authenticity of the
latter, as theologians tended to do. During the heyday
of Neo-Orthodoxy he did not get much of a hearing.

Now, in view of this divergence of types in the
experience of civilized humanity, Tyrrell's failure to see
Jesus as the culmination of the prophetic line and his
tendency to make a mystic out of him appeared to Söderblom
as a dangerous confusion of categories. Tyrrell, von
Hügel and the Catholic Modernists generally tended to
see even the Christian religion as ultimately mystical,
not realizing that there was an alternative. An apprecia-
tion of Luther was sorely needed. Luther represented a
renewal of distinctly revelational religion and of the
personality-affirming type of intense religious experience,
and that in a fullness which ruled out any rationalistic
watering-down of the reality of the living God. In turn-
ing his back on the ascetic practices of the monks and on
the ecstatic states and raptures of the mystics, he was
not fragmenting the Christian whole, as the Modernists
held, but abandoning religious elements which were adven-
titious to Christianity and recalling Christianity to its
own historic heritage: the life of personal love and action
face to face with the God revealed in a person, Jesus
Christ.

As if in answer to Tyrrell's plea for scientific
enlightenment, Söderblom pointed out that there is a type
of religion which carries the moral struggle between good
and evil into the most sublime reaches of communion with
God. Such is Christianity, in which God personally gives
his pledge of salvation and enlists the believer in a

fuller life by coupling love of neighbor and loyalty to Himself indissolubly together. With the centrality of personality in biblical religion goes the sense for history. Here Jesus typified the prophetical emphasis on the divine as a living will determined to bring good out of the world process. Söderblom discerned a striking correlation between these characteristics of biblical religion and contemporary philosophical thinking, such as Bergson's *evolution creatrice*. For this philosophical side of the matter, however, we must content ourselves here with a reference to *Religionsproblemet* (1910a, pp. 136-61) and *The Living God* (1933, pp. 310-11).

In a typically Catholic fashion, Tyrrell combined the mystical and prophetic types of religiosity without suspecting the distinctiveness of the latter. Had he done so, he would not necessarily have been obliged to disown the mystical tradition ruthlessly (Söderblom nowhere went so far as to insist on this), but he could have asserted the primacy of the personal, the historical, and the role of conscience more effectively. He might also have spared Christianity in its regrettably divided state another dose of interconfessional polemics. The reforms he strove for were undercut by the Plotinian mystical ideal of beatitude to which he still paid tribute. For it depressed the personal element and the importance of historical existence to the benefit of the institutional and impersonal dimensions of Catholicism under which Tyrrell had so much to endure.

Conclusion

Söderblom's *Religionsproblemet* may be responsible in

some cases and to some extent for the interest of Scandi-
navian Lutherans for ecumenical dialogue with Catholics,
but it could have been written in runes for all the impact
it made on the Catholic partners in the dialogue. The
only Catholic who can be shown to have read this book,
unfortunately never translated, was Friedrich Heiler; it
was instrumental in his passage to a sort of Catholic
Lutheranism (Misner, ed.).[8] Of course, any adherents of
Modernism left in the Roman Catholic fold after 1910 were
reduced to silence, so there could be no public exchange
on the subject. One wonders, nevertheless, how a Laber-
thonnière, for instance, would have responded to Söderblom's constructive criticism, had the book been translated.

This brief sample of the method and content of
Söderblom's discussion of the Modernist movement may suffice at any rate to make plausible the assertion, that
Religionsproblemet ranks with the efforts of Paul Sabatier,
Ernst Troetsch, Adolf von Harnack and Newman Smyth to
come to a better understanding of modern Roman Catholicism
in the years preceding World War I. It may be true by
now, as Hans Küng claims, that the "'Catholic' and 'Protestant' basic attitudes are by no means mutually exclusive" and that innumerable Christians "do in fact live out
an evangelical catholicity centered on the Gospel or a
catholic evangelicity maintaining a Catholic breadth of
vision."[9] If this is so, it is certainly due in part
to the influence of the Lutheran scholar and archbishop,
Nathan Söderblom, who did all in his power to include
Roman Catholicism in his ecumenical thinking and acting.
It is also due to his measure to the ardent Modernist,
who spread an ideal of catholicism within and far beyond
his confessional boundaries (Tyrrell lies buried in

Storrington, as Abbé Bremond noted, "halfway between the two Churches, the one in which he died and the other in which he was born" Petre 1912, II, 443). It is only to be regretted that Söderblom's pages should have gone unnoticed on the part of Roman Catholics for two-thirds of a century of ecumenical endeavours.

Notes

[1]I will follow the practice of giving short references (author, year, page numbers) within the text and of
providing full publication date once only here in the
notes. A great deal of research on Tyrrell has been completed or is under way, but not much of it has been published as yet. The special focus of this investigation
is his posthumous work, *Christianity at the Cross-Roads*
(London: Longmans Green, 1909; cited here according to
the ed. by A. R. Vidler, London: Allen & Unwin, 1963).
Other works in regard to Tyrrell are: Maude D. Petre,
Autobiography and Life of George Tyrrell, 2 vols. (London:
Arnold, 1912); by the same, *Von Hügel and Tyrrell: The
Story of a Friendship* (London: Dent, 1937); A. R. Vidler,
The Modernist Movement in the Roman Chruch (Cambridge:
University Press, 1934); John Ratté, *Three Modernists:
Alfred Loisy, George Tyrrell, William L. Sullivan* (New
York: Sheed & Ward, 1967); and Bruno Faupel, *Die Religion-
sphilosophie George Tyrrells*, (Freiburg: Herder, 1976).
    Two works of Söderblom provide comment on Tyrrell's
treatment of the question of the historical Jesus:
Religionsproblemet inom katolicism och protestantism
(Stockholm: Geber, 1910 [1910a]) and "Jesus eller Kristus?"
(1910b) in *När stunderna växla och skrida*, 2d ed., (Stock-
holm: Diakonstyrelses Bokförlag, 1935), I, pp. 275-301.
Among his other works we note: *La vie future d'après le
Mazdeisme* (Paris: Laroux, 1901); *The Nature of Revelation*
(1903), tr. F. E. Pamp (New York: Oxford University Press,
1933); and *The Living God* (1933) (rpt. Boston: Beacon
Press, 1962). Important secondary literature: Bengt

Sundkler, *Nathan Söderblom: His Life and Work* (London:
Lutterworth, 1968); Hans Akerberg,*Omvandelse och kamp* . . .
Nathan Söderbloms religiöse utveckling 1866-1894, (Lund:
Studentlitteratur, 1975; with summary in English, pp.
284-322); and Eric J. Sharpe, *Comparative Religion: A
History,* (New York: Scribner, 1975). Letters to each
other by Söderblom and von Hügel may be consulted in my
edition: Friedrich von Hügel--Nathan Söderblom--Friedrich
Heiler, *Briefwechsel 1909-1931* (Paderborn: Bonifacius,
1977).

[2]Johannes Weiss, *Jesus' Proclamation of the Kingdom
of God,* tr. and ed. with introd. by R. H. Heirs and D. L.
Holland, (Philadelphia: Fortress Press, 1971 [1892]);
Alfred Loisy, *The Gospel and the Church,* tr. C. Home, ed.
with introd. by B. B. Scott, (Philadelphia: Fortress
Press, 1976 [1902]); both are in the Lives of Jesus Series,
Leander E. Keck, general editor. Loisy's book was a
refutation of Adolf von Harnack, *What is Christianity?
(Das Wesen des Christentums,* 1900), tr. T. B. Saunders
(New York: Harper, 1957). In 1906 Albert Schweitzer
published his famous work on the question, *Von Reimarus
zu Wrede,* tr. as *The Quest of the Historical Jesus* in
1910.

[3]Indications are that Weiss's work played no special
role in the formation of Loisy's view of the historical
Jesus; cf. Loisy, *Mémoires pour servir a l'histoire
religieuse de notre temps* (Paris: Nourry, 1930-31), I,
pp. 121, 147-55, 443-44 (Letter to von Hügel of 8 August
1897).

[4]Cf. Pietro Scoppola, *Crisi modernista e rinnova-
mento cattolico in Italia,* 3d ed. (Bologna: II Mulino,
1975), p. 292; Emile Poulat, *Histoire, dogme et critique*

dans la crise moderniste, (Tournai: Casterman, 1962); and *Au coeur de la crise moderniste: le dossier inédit d'une controverse,* with introd. and "postface" by René Marlé (Paris: Aubier, 1960); the reaction of the magisterium: Denzinger and Schönmeister, *Enchiridion Symbolorum,* 33d ed. (1965), nos. 3401-3500 and 3537-3550, esp. propositions 31-34 condemned in the decree *Lamentabili* of 3 July 1907.

[5]Literature in Christian Schütz, *Mysterium Salutis,* V (Einsiedeln: Benziger, 1976), p. 617.

[6]Söderblom can be seen as an early exemplification of "Christian transcultural consciousness" in the sense of William M. Thompson, "The Risen Christ, Transcultural Consciousness, and the Encounter of the World Religions," *Theological Studies,* 37 (1976), pp. 381-409.

[7]Fredrich Heiler, *Prayer,* tr. S. McComb (New York: Oxford University Press, 1932), pp. 135-71.

[8]See also Misner, *"Religio Eruditi,"* Journal of the American Academy of Religion, 45 Supplement (September 1977). There is one other case where a Catholic may have read *Religionsproblemet:* in late 1927 and early 1928 some Catholic newspapers in Germany published a scurrilous attack on Söderblom, supposedly based on it, cf. Misner, ed., letters no. 82 and 83.

[9]Hans Küng, *To Be a Christian,* tr. E. Quinn (Garden City, N.Y.: Doubleday, 1976), p. 502.

TOWARD A CHRISTIAN BIBLICAL ETHIC

Robert J. Daly, S.J.

When we take up the task of working out a method for doing New Testament ethics, i.e., Christian ethics for today done from the perspective of and fully consistent with Christian biblical faith, we inevitably become involved in an intensely systematic task. It is the task of developing an integral Christian ethic. But Christian ethics cannot be integral unless thay make full use of the humane and social sciences as well as of theological and biblical scholarship. Thus, if anything significant is to be accomplished in this direction, a team approach will obviously be necessary. This essay will summarize the results of one such attempt, now moving into its third year, to stimulate the kind of team approach which the development of an integral Christian ethic seems to require.[1]

A detailed description of our ultimate goal can be given by expanding on the implications of the task formulated in the first sentence of this essay. Its concern lies in *doing* Christian ethics, i.e., with working out and actually applying practical principles of Christian living. Its concern lies in doing *Christian* ethics i.e., the practical principles of Christian existence or life in Christ. By *ethics* is understood the task of working out modes of moral reasoning which will be true rational expressions of the principles of right human behavior and activity. *From the perspective of and fully consistent with* Christian biblical faith, refers to the task of drawing upon the values, ideals, goals, directions and teachings of the Bible (as fulfilled in the New Testament) and Christian life, and of integrating these values, ideals, etc. into ethics. *Christian* biblical *faith* refers to the mode of existence of those who are in Christ. *Biblical* refers more specifically to the mode(s) of practical moral existence revealed to us in the Bible, in a centrally unique way in the Christ-event, and in a continuing way through the Spirit of Christ in the life of the church.[2]

Since the ultimate goal is to work out a method for actually *doing* Christian biblical ethics, as explained above, to establish a methodology for studying the ethics contained in the New Testament writings is insufficient. The historical-critical method already has this task reasonably well in hand; and the results it is achieving are obviously foundational for our work. However, critical exegesis does not in itself possess adequate methods for completing the foundation needed for building an integral Christian ethics. Exegesis alone is not up to the task of studying the ethics of the New Testament as a whole. It seems that this can be achieved only when exegesis is complemented by a coherent theological perspective which is grounded in Christian existence. This means that the existential hermeneutical center for doing Christian biblical ethics is our own contemporary experience of life in Christ--just as the existential hermeneutical center out of which the New Testament authors conceived their ethical concepts and teachings was their own experience of life in Christ, their own *Sitz im Leben*.

There are two major levels on which this has to be

approached: the biblical level and the systematic level.
On the biblical level there are, first, the specifically
exegetical (but also hermeneutical) tasks of identifying
and investigating those passages and aspects of the New
Testament which have ethical content or relevance (which
is not to suggest that only passages which can be identified as ethical or exhortatory need be considered). Then
there is the methodological or hermeneutical task of arti-
culating an over-arching method, context, or organizational
principle within which the specifically exegetical tasks
can contribute more productively to the ultimate goal.
On the systematic level there is the task which, in the
age of specialization, is as difficult as it is necessary:
the task of beginning to build the bridges to the other
theological and academic disciplines which will be needed
in order to begin doing Christian ethics for today from
the perspective of and fully consistent with Christian
biblical faith.

This article will have three parts: 1) a brief
description of some of the exegetical problems involved
with doing New Testament ethics; 2) a discussion of the
dogmatic and systematic implications of this task; 3) an
attempt, first, to describe more fully the existential
context of doing New Testament ethics, and then to cate-
gorize and list the major tasks of approaches.

Exegetical Problems

The unity and plurality of the New Testament and of
its ethics in particular, is one of the first problems to
be faced. There are two basic approaches. The first is
to study each New Testament work or identifiable unit

individually, on its own terms. This can indeed give us
the ethics of John, or of Paul, etc., but no one of these
represents the fullness of New Testament ethical teaching.[3]
The second approach is to synthesize the ethical aspects
of the various New Testament documents into a unified
teaching. When used alone, the inadequacy of the first
approach for doing Christian biblical ethics is obvious;
but on the other hand, the illegitimacy of the harmoniza-
tions needed by the second approach has long been recognized. Nevertheless, if we are to proceed with our task,
ways of integrating the two approaches must be found.

H. D. Wendland's attempt to do this has produced some
significant results. After studying the ethical teaching
of the New Testament authors one by one according to the
principles of critical exegesis, he concludes with a brief
attempt at the second approach and finds four aspects of
New Testament ethics present in all the major New Testament
writings. These are: 1) the love command, 2) a critical
relationship to the world, 3) ethics of the community for
the community, 4) the interrelationship of eschatology
and ethics.[4] Few could have any difficulty in accepting
these conclusions--except to marvel at how jejune they
are. Where are Jesus Christ, Servant Christology and
the imitation of Christ? What about sin and death, and
the transforming power of Jesus' death and resurrection?
What about the reality and consequences of our being
baptized into Jesus' death and resurrection?

It is indeed significant that Wendland's results
are so minimalist. However, this does not imply that he
himself is a minimalist or that he proceeds from reduc-
tionist presuppositions. What it does indicate is that
critical exegesis, when limited to its own resources,

cannot alone formulate adequate principles of Christian
biblical ethics.

Systematic Implications

Theology therefore, as well as exegesis, has a
bearing on the task.[5] Three major questions can be asked:
1) Is there a Christian ethics? 2) Is there an ethics
in the New Testament (or in the Bible as a whole)? 3) Is
there a Christian biblical ethics? With proper qualifica-
tions, all three questions can be answered affirmatively.
Many, however, disagree. Apart from terminological problems, much of this disagreement is due to serious differences in theology and belief. In fact, almost all that
one holds as a theologian or believes as a Christian
inevitably influences one's concepts and conclusions when
the question of Christian biblical ethics is raised.

J. Gustafson tries to answer the question "Can
ethics be Christian?"[6] by asking the question: "Are
there moral actions that are mandatory for religious
persons only for 'religious' or 'Christian' reasons and
not for reasons on which all rational persons could presumably agree?" (p. 146). If the answer is yes, then
presumably there is a Christian ethics. Scripture is used
in all the various ways in which Gustafson indicates a
Christian might answer this question. But precisely how
is scripture used, and with what authority? Gustafson
is basically correct in answering:

> What gives the scripture some authority for us is
> neither a fundamentalistic view nor the view that
> an ecclesiastical decision was made to close the
> canon, but rather that the perceptions of the
> meaning of God's presence recorded there are to

> some extent confirmed in our current experience
> in the Christian and wider community. . . . The
> central symbol for Christians historically has
> been Jesus Christ (*Can Ethics Be Christian?*, p.
> 161).

From this, two central issues emerge: 1) the hermeneutical question of circularity, and 2) the largely exegetical but also theological question of the accessibility of the central Christian symbol, Jesus Christ. In various ways, these two issues affect almost every aspect of this project.

Gustafson answers his basic question by claiming to prove that Christian ethics cannot be converted into "natural" or "rational" ethics without remainder (*Can Ethics Be Christian?*, p. 164). Although this article supports this conclusion, the question is not well phrased. In putting it this way, Gustafson is, as it were, standing outside the Christian "conspiracy." He may thereby escape the Christian hermeneutical circle, but only by inserting himself into another, nonChristian or "rational" hermeneutical circle. From within the nonChristian circle there is no way of adequately coming to terms with what many Christians perceive to be the very foundation and vital source of Christian moral existence: the ontic (not just symbolic) reality of the Christian's incorporation into Christ. As Birch and Rasmussen put it (pp. 80-82), the ethics of *doing* is dependent on the ethics of *being*. Who a Christian *is* determines *what* a Christian *does*. In traditional scholastic terms, *agere sequitur esse*; (activity follows upon being). Christian faith or biblical ethics is a matter of *agere sequitur* Christian *esse*, and this Christian being or existence is created by Christian faith or believing.

But a defensive posture, as suggested by the question "Can ethics be Christian?" with Christian ethics standing, as it were, at the house of rational ethics with hat in hand asking to be let in, should be rejected. It is better to move to the "attack" and make the claim that for ethics to be truly ethics, or to be truly human and integral, it must also be Christian.

The formation of an integral Christian biblical ethics will be feasible only when a group (community) of Christians is looking toward its central symbol, Jesus Christ, and to the New Testament as the personal source of its understanding of Jesus Christ. That community will then be able to articulate action-guiding principles and values and their justifications in terms which are both religious and rational and which are adequate to the realities and the ideals of Christian existence. Since biblical studies do not in themselves have the unity and system which is needed for an adequate formulation of this kind, aid is needed from systematics. Inevitably, therefore, a choice must be made between different theologies and, in doing so, the inquirer's hermeneutical principles will make critical control very difficult. To illustrate what is involved here, Aristotle's view of the end or goal of human existence will be contrasted with the goal of human existence as seen through the biblical Christian view. Aristotle does not, of course fully represent "rational ethics." He is simply a convenient example, an example which might be particularly helpful because of the recent revival of interest in character and virtue among contemporary moral philosophers and Christian ethicists.[7]

In the first book of the *Nicomachean Ethics*, Aristotle begins by pointing out that all things tend toward

their own ends, and that the end to which all things
tend is the good; that the highest good for man is that
which in the realm of action is desired for its own sake
and which determines all our other desires; that the common good is higher than the individual good; that the
highest good attainable by action is happiness; that happiness is defined as activity in conformity with virtue
in a complete life; and that the highest virtue is con-
templation. The perfect fulfillment of this highest
virtue seems to be basically immanent.

When a Christian begins to express the goal of Christian existence, he/she may well find that he can use the
same basic teleological structure as Aristotle; he will
be able to affirm practically all that Aristotle does, but
all along the way he will find that his teleological
understanding of Christian existence goes beyond and transcends Aristotle's. The Christian is aware that the fundamental teleology in things is due to God's creation and
providence; that all things are good precisely because
created by God; that man and woman are the center of
creation (in God's image and likeness) and therefore good
in a preeminent way; that all other things are subordinate
to man and woman, but that sin has flawed the goodness of
this creation and introduced patterns and cycles of sin
and decline; that Jesus however redeemed us and enabled
us to share in his victory over sin and death; that the
dynamic of this redemption introduces transcendent, Christic patterns of triumph over sin, which patterns we call
the "Law of the Cross," or the "Paschal Mystery"; that
the common good is rooted in the community of saints;
that the highest good is not a this-worldly happiness,
but a transcendent blessedness or sanctity; that blessedness

is the active living of Christian community life in this life *and* in the next; and that, finally, the active living of the Christian life is life in Jesus Christ.

Where Aristotle goes on to talk about virtue in general, and then the particular virtues by which the good life is lived, the Christian goes on to speak about living, qua member of the communion of saints, the primary theological virtues of faith, hope and love, and in the context of these three, the cardinal and moral virtues. But all the while, the Christian is aware that he is talking about life in Jesus Christ, and that everything centers around the relationship of one's personal and community existence to the central Christian symbol, Jesus Christ. While for Aristotle the ultimate ethical norm is wholly immanent, for the Christian, the nature of man and therefore the ultimate ethical norm are both immanent and transcendent: they are grounded in the individual person, both human and divine, Jesus Christ,[8] with whom we are united, into whom we are ontically incorporated, in whose nature--consubstantial with the Father--we share.

If then, for the sake of ethical communality, the Christian agrees with the rational ethicist to build a common ethics based on the nature of the human person, the very validity of the venture must first be questioned on the grounds that they may not indeed be talking about the same thing. If Christian existence is so different from purely rational or purely human existence, how can we build a common ethics? But the supernatural existential which Henri de Lubac and Karl Rahner spoke about suggests that all human beings, whether they are conscious of it or not, have an openness towards or potential for approaching God. Christians as opposed to those without

a faith ethic, may be much closer to each other in terms
of foundations for a common ethic than theologians often
suppose. The Aristotelian *Weltanschauung* is created by
Aristotelian *credere*, much in the same way that the Christian world-view is created by Christian belief. This, of
course, raises the question whether there really is such
a thing as non-faith ethics. I am reminded of the statement Bernard Lonergan, S.J. is fond of repeating: "Ninety-
five percent of what a genius knows he knows by faith."
For these reasons, and also because I am personally convinced (my own *credere*) that grace does indeed build on
nature, that is not only created in God's image and likeness but also possesses an ontological opening to sharing
in the divine life, I have to profess myself optimistic
at least about the possibility of Christians and non-
Christians working out a common ethic.

Nevertheless, there is a qualitiativly superior
relationship for Christian faith ethics over non-faith
ethics (i.e., over ethics which profess themselves to be
merely natural, human or rational).[9] This needs to be
followed immediately with two important qualifying remarks:
1) it is almost impossible to make this affirmation in
such a way as to avoid the myraid misunderstandings to
which it is prone. 2) Every Christian ethicist must be
willing to make this or a similar affirmation.

Since many ethicists will either reject or feel
uncomfortable with this affirmation and its second qualifying statement, this position must be butressed. Its
defense centers around the problem of moral impotence.
As Paul, Ovid and Augustine knew well, and as Rousseau in
his First Discourse had to remind the fathers of the
Enlightenment, there is a great difference, sometimes a

chasm, between knowing the good and being able to do it. Knowledge simply does not equal virtue.

The Gospel teaching on nonviolence can serve as an example. If it is "an incontestable fact that Christ did preach nonviolence, both as a condition and a consequence of the universal love he taught us,"[10] Christians will obviously feel obliged to live accordingly. One who professes adherence to merely natural, human or rational ethics could, of course, by reason alone, come to the same conclusion. However, when it comes to living up to this conviction, in the moment of truth when adherence to nonviolent principles may mean persecution or even martyrdom, the Christian will probably have access to far greater resources than the mere humanist. The Christian who is aware that the truest and deepest reaches of his being lies in incorporation into the suffering and risen Christ, who realizes that death is the door to eternal life, who realizes that martyrdom is the way to the closest personal union with Jesus Christ--this person is aware of having access to resources which transcend the merely human, and which will help him face the varying degrees of *kenosis* which a commitment to nonviolence will often entail. On the other hand, the person without religious faith, unaware of a personal call to be baptized into the death and resurrection of Jesus, who has not meditated on the Paschal Mystery and the Law of the Cross, however noble and elevated such persons may judge kenotic martyrdom to be, they will hardly be able to accept it as readily as the devout Christian.

This leads directly to what is meant by Jesus Christ as the central Christian symbol, and to the question of the accessibility of this symbol. Since Christian

existence lies in Christ, symbol is used not just in a
merely logical sense, but above all in the ontological
sense (common in traditional Catholic sacramental theology) in which the symbol effectively brings about and
is in some way really identified with what it symbolizes.

This understood, the central issue becomes: How
do men have access to/become identified with Jesus Christ?
This can take place in two distinguishable but inter-
related ways: 1) personal, existential appropriation by
way of entering into the life of Christ. This seems to
eliminate the possibility of clearly defined boundaries
between Christian faith, ethics and spiritual theology.
The one ineveitably involves, and cannot be complete without, the other. 2) The second way is that of cognitional
appropriation by means of historical knowledge about Jesus.
This involves us in the problem of the historical Jesus.[11]
It also involves us in the problematic of contemporary
historiography which judges fully objective history to be
impossible. Unable to escape our own hermeneutical
circles, we must try to use them to our advantage.[12] We
thus approach the New Testament, already "knowing" what
we are looking for. It might be helpful here to remember
that such a bias is not the deadly sin of scholarship;
that particular deadly sin is rather blindness to important things which are there, and a perverse insistence
on finding things which are not there. However, the best
protection against such blindness and perversity, and the
best means to turn individual and group bias to profit,
is a humble attitude of dialogue with those who approach
matters from different methodological, theological and
faith perspectives.

The fundamental question remains: "Is there, or,

is it possible to work out a Christian biblical ethic
suitable for today?" This requires a nuanced response.
The fundamental attitudes, values, even principles of a
Christian ethical system are present in the New Testament.
Exegetes can even agree on some salient common features in
the ethics found in the New Testament authors. But for
more than this, for anything approaching a usable ethical
system, we look in vain. It is for Christians in their
own milieu, like Paul in his letters, to meditate on the
values, attitudes and "principles" expressed and mediated
by the central Christian symbol, Jesus Christ, in order
from that source and in their own context to work out
their Christian biblical ethics. This task is simultaneously exegetical, theological, and existential-spiri-
tual. Only when it is attempted in humble dialogue and
with continued vigilance regarding both the dangers and
opportunities presented by individual and group biases,
can both the pernicious anemia of irrelevance and the
deadly sins of blindness to evidence and eisegetical
perversity be avoided.

How, then, can a method for doing Christian biblical ethics be sketched? (If, in so doing, the New
Testament is used rather more than the Bible as a whole,
it is because that is where the Old Testament finds
its fulfillment; and that is where, of course, Jesus
Christ, the central Christian symbol, is most clearly
accessible to us.) First our own *Sitz im Leben* (existential situation in life) in doing Christian/New Testament ethics must be located and described. This centers
around our individual and communal *access* to Jesus Christ,
and the effect of this access on individual and community.
This access, as already noted, is achieved by the inter-

related and interdependent means: 1) of our individual and communal *historical* continuity with Jesus, and 2) of our *metahistorical* (existential or sacramental) incorporation into Christ through the mediation/ministry of the Christian community guided by Christ's Spirit.

The Christian biblical ethicist, therefore, must try to come to terms with several worlds of meaning. The most important of these are, 1) the biblical world of the Ancient Near East and Eastern Mediterranean Basin--primarily a task for biblical scholarship, and 2) the existential world of the contemporary Christian--primarily a task for the theologian and ethicist. In brief, the sources come from the classical world of the ancients and the contemporary world.[13]

When we apply the perspectives of these two worlds to a foundational ethical problem such as moral impotence, some illuminating similarities and divergences appear. Paul's experience and description (in Romans) of the problem of moral impotence is not unlike that of the early moderns (Machiavelli, Hobbes, Locke) and later moderns (Marx, Nietzsche, Freud). But Paul's solution diverges from that of the moderns and is similar to that of the ancients (Plato and Aristotle), but with one crucial difference.

Paul agrees with the moderns in seeing human nature as a congeries of selfish drives. This is a "low" view of humanity in which man in unable to control or transcend his inclination to the bad (the ancients) or his natural (i.e., animal) selfish instincts (the moderns). But here, Paul parts with the moderns who believe the only solution is to lower the standards and make the best of our evil inclinations, and seems to side with the more

optimistic ancients who believed that by the cultivation
of reasonable virtue man could rise somewhat above the
material, animal level of human existence and, by personal
and communal assimilation to the Good, achieve the good
life. Now the crucial difference: Paul is aware that
Christians achieve the good life not by realizing their
natural potential but by being *transformed* (cf. Rom 12:
1-2) and by being incorporated--really and not just sym-
bolically--into the life of Jesus. Christians accept the
Law of the Cross and are taken up into the Paschal Mystery.

Theologically speaking, this means that grace is not
only saving, it is also elevating. It brings us to a new
mode of existence: life in Christ. This elevation is
characterized functionally by the special and unique ways,
the specifically Christic ways, of grappling with human
bias and moral impotence. These Christic ways (the Law
of the Cross and the Paschal Mystery) of grappling with
material and personal evil lead to the good life not in
the Greek sense (as described above when speaking of
Aristotle), but in the transformative, Christian sense.
This makes possible--but by God's power, not ours--what
the ancients could conceptualize but, as Augustine showed,
could not realize, and what the moderns did not even think
was possible: the good life for man.[14]

This means that between rational ethics and faith
ethics there is both a continuity and a discontinuity.
In theological terms, the continuity can be expressed in
the affirmation that grace does not supplant but builds
upon nature, while the discontinuity can be expressed in
the Augustinian and Thomistic insights into the gratuity
of grace and the distinction between the orders of faith

and reason, grace and nature. In experiential or practical
ethical terms, the continuity is experienced when men and
women of different allegiances reason and work together
towards attaining the good life, while the discontinuity
is experienced when they are called on to make mature,
responsible ethical decisions (e.g., regarding acts of
kenotic, martyrial self-giving) for reasons which transcend
the dynamic of rational or merely natural ethics. Paul
spoke of this as the difference between life lived on the
level of the flesh (*sarx*) and on the level of the Spirit
(*pneuma*). On this level, decisions and actions seem
necessarily to involve a trans-rational process which is
both continuous with rational ethics (the natural level
on which elevating grace builds) and discontinuous with
it (because elevating grace transcends nature).

Existential Context of New Testament Ethics

Before going on to make a few suggestions on how
a group of scholars might go about the common task of
doing Christian biblical ethics, the central Christian
symbol, Jesus Christ, and the unique communication of
that symbol, the New Testament must be reexamined in an
attempt to discover how ethical living--more specifically,
Christian existence--is preached or communicated by Jesus
Christ himself, by the New Testament, and by the Christian faith communities of the past and present. Four
modes of communication (perhaps more, or others) can be
distinguished: the indicative, the imperative, the parabolic, and the mystical.

-(1) In the *indicative mode* the story of salvation
history is told. This apparently simple statement

is, however, in its implications, as complicated and
as vast as all knowable reality. Although it is a
story that has its center in biblical revelation
and the Gospel (the story about Jesus Christ),
it is also a continuing story that both antedates
and will postdate all human history. And it is
also a story in which we all have a part.

-(2) In the *imperative mode*, the various books of
the Old and New Testaments, and Jesus himself in
the Gospels, prescribe certain things to do or not
do. All of these prescriptions are part of the
ongoing story of salvation history, and none of them
can be separated from their place in the story. Some
of them have obviously been superseded because the
story has moved on to another stage. Others (speaking of biblical imperatives) retain all or part of
their prescriptive validity for us to the extent
that the story in which they have their setting
remains or has become our story. Still other imperatives, ones not contained explicitly in the biblical story, have prescriptive value for us because
they have a place in our own story within the full
story of salvation history. In other words, salvation history supplies the medium of continuity
between biblical imperatives and post-biblical
Christian imperatives. The import of this remark
is to remind us that it is not the fact of a bil-
lical imperative nor its source (e.g., reported as
the words of Christ) that gives it its prescriptive
value, but rather its place in the story of salvation history and its relation to our individual
and communal places in that story. This does not

reduce to situation ethics, as a superficial and
hostile interpretation might suggest, but it does
explain why Christians today, who have become aware
of historicity as well as salvation history, are
comfortable with far fewer moral absolutes than
their forebears in faith. Nor does this reduce to
an individualistic ethic with each one deciding
individually just where he fits into the story of
salvation history. For ethics to be Christian it
must always remain what is true of all New Testament
ethics: it is an ethic of the community and for
the community. It is from within and only from
within the broad context of salvation history and
the more particular context of our own chruch community that one can begin to interpret and apply
correctly the different kinds of moral imperatives,
exhortations and counsels of the Bible.

-(3) In the *parabolic mode*, the Gospels report Jesus
as preaching or communicating his "moral message,"
his "way," i.e., Christian existence, in parables.
These are with *stories within a story*. Already
having a place in the story of salvation history,
we are challenged to enter psychologically or imagina-
tively into the story of the parable in order to
enable ourselves to enter more profoundly or more
completely into salvation history (which for us is
our own existential--both individual and communal--
entering into a life of Christ). Of great significance here, in the light of the discontinuity already
discussed between faith ethics and rational ethics,
is the fact that the parable, characteristically,
can neither be allegorized nor rationally explained

without losing much of its essential dynamism. The
dynamism of a parable transcends rational ethics in
two ways: 1) one cannot conceptualize or rationally
explain a parable without "killing" it, and 2) what
the parable effects (our fuller incorporation into
Christ) transcends the natural level and thus the
merely rational means of dealing with it.[15]

It may be well to remind ourselves at this point how
effective "telling a story" has been not only as a means
of religious and ethical teaching, but also as an efficient
catalyst for ethical commitment and action. Story telling
has always been one of the favorite and most effective
tools of the preacher. The stories are sometimes distinctly religious, hagiographical or moralizing; they are
also at times, like the parables of Jesus, non-sacral or
non-religious in their specific material content. The
ability to tell a good story is one of the marks of a good
preacher or speaker. The Christian preacher has the story
of Jesus Christ to tell. This is the insight which pierces
through the cliché of the title: "The Greatest Story Ever
Told."

Since story and parable are primary means of access
to Jesus Christ, the central Christian symbol, their role
in the dynamic of rational ethics and faith ethics should
be considered. In this dynamic we can distinguish three
phases:

- (a) The *first phase* in the dynamic of the parabolic
mode establishes the foundations, principles, values
and goals of one's ethical mode of existence. For
Christian or faith-ethical existence, this foundational *Weltanschauung* is mediated to us primarily
by means of story, the story of salvation history.

Because this story is the Word of God as well as of
man, the process of coming to know and enter into
this story involves both faith and reason. For
rational-ethical existence, the foundational
Weltanschauung is mediated to us primarily by our
analytic reason and human experience. Story may
play an important role, as in the myths of Plato,
but the process does not become transcendent; it
remains a human one carried out with human capaci-
ties.

-(b) The *second phase* in the dynamic of the parabolic
mode is the one of applying this *Weltanschauung* to
one's concrete, practical mode of existence. Rational
ethics will do this characteristically by means of
deduction and inference. Christian faith-ethics will
use these same rational means, but will characteristically rely both on a general appeal to the place
this particular situation has in the large story
of salvation history, and on a paritcular use of
parable (story within the story) to illuminate
the concrete practical situation. Rational ethics
can make a similar use of story and parable, but
it has in itself, apart from faith ethics, no means
of access to the transcendent dynamism of the faith-
ethical process. Rational ethics, then, left to
its own resources, might well come to the conclusion that there is no such thing as Christian ethics
which is distinct from and more than rational or
merely human ethics.

-(c) The *third phase* in the dynamic of the parabolic
mode involves the application and realization of the
first two phases to concrete human situations. It

is the final stage of decision and commitment which
(to use Lonergan's scheme) follows on the preliminary ones of experiencing, understanding and judging.
This is the phase where rational ethics becomes
particularly inadequate and where faith-ethics
makes an increased use of story and parable. The
problem is not merely to *know* the good. Although
it cannot do as complete a job as faith-ethics,
rational ethics can be quite helpful in this. But
the really difficult problem, the one in which
rational ethics alone is of very little help, is to
transcend one's individual and communal moral impotence and find the wherewithal actually to do the
good. We achieve this by existentially entering
into the story of salvation history. This leads
to the fourth mode in which Christian existence is
communicated by Jesus Christ, the New Testament, and
the living Christian communities: the mystical mode.
-(4) In the *mystical mode*, the actuality of Christian
existence is (at least partially, or inceptively)
realized, i.e., the Christian enters, or enters more
fully, into Christ. The first three modes (indicative, imperative and parabolic), although they
have aspects which are existentially contemporary,
focus on the center of the story of salvation history: Jesus and the New Testament. But the mystical
mode, while remaining in continuity with the other
three, focuses nevertheless on what is taking place
now: our individual and communal incorporation
into Christ. This comprises the whole panoply of
experiences and realities, whether "mystical" or
not, which we variously call: discernment,

spiritual illumination, individual or community
"inspiration," prophecy, visions, or just simply
acquiring the mind of Christ or "growing up in
Christ," i.e., advancing "in wisdom and in stature,
and in favor with God and man" (Luke 2:52). This,
and only this, represents the crowning and completion of the Christian ethical process. Here, at
its completion, Christian ethics becomes indistin-
guishable from spirituality.

Although we can conceptually distinguish these four
modes, functionally they are never completely separate from
each other. The Christian who listens to the story, hear-
kens to the commands, and enters into the parables of
Jesus is the same Christian who has been and is being incorporated into Christ.

Conclusion

Up to this point, this essay has been an attempt to
set the stage for doing Christian biblical ethics. However, even apart from the limitations of any one person
or group of persons, it is a stage which can never be set
perfectly or completely. For the action which takes place
on that stage is divine and human together: the continuing story of salvation. The general ethical task is to
study what is transpiring on that stage in order to enter
into it more completely. The particular task now at hand
is to study the New Testament aspects of what is going on
there. Exegetical and biblical research must, however, be
pursued in conjunction with other theological and related
disciplines. The findings of these studies might well
modify, improve, or even challenge our foundational

overview. But this is as it should be. Only if by remaining open to this continuing modification and correction
can the scholar overcome the limitations of and make the
most advantageous use of the potentialities of the hermeneutical and methodological circles within which he works.

The particular tasks which the New Testament
scholars have in this total project can be divided into
three groups: 1) the study of an individual work or
author or related group of works in the New Testament;
2) the study of particular aspects or approaches to New
Testament ethics; 3) the study of particular ethical
topics or problems which may be present in several or
even most of the works in the New Testament.

   -(1) The study of an individual work, author, or
   related group of works in the New Testament is one
   area in which there already exists some consensus
   in critical exegesis. However, satisfactory methods
   of "harmonizing" or even helpfully interrelating
   the results of such studies with each other and with
   the rest of the New Testament--to say nothing of
   Christian life itself--must be worked out as well
   as possible in order to meet the existential needs
   of those trying to do Christian biblical ethics.
   Further extensive subdivisions of this grouping
   become necessary when in undertaking the study of
   particular ethical topics (group 3) or of particular
   aspects of approaches (group 2) within an individual work or author (group 1). One can remark in
   general that the methodological and hermeneutical
   difficulty increases as does the scope of the unit
   studied.

   -(2) The study of particular aspects or approaches
   to New Testament ethics may well be at present   the

most fruitful general area of investigation. For
one thing, studies of this kind are not necessarily
closely dependent on a total foundational overview; and even when one's overview proves to be
inadequate or incorrect, the results one has achieved
are not affected as much as would be the case if
one were studying a particular ethical topic (group
3). Even partially correct results can still contribute usefully to the modification and expansion
of one's whole foundational overview. Some areas for
investigation under this grouping would be: the
function of story and/or parable as a means of communicating ethical knowledge and stimulating ethical
commitment; the kinds and functions of the commands
and precepts (cf. imperative mode) in the New Testament, especially compared with other biblical,
Judaic and contemporary sources; the mystical mode
of Christian life as a means of communicating ethical knowledge and stimulating ethical commitment;
the continuity and discontinuity of rational and
faith ethics in the New Testament in general, or
in some part of it such as the preaching of Jesus
or the moral exhortations of Paul; the Christian
community itself as a medium of communicating knowledge and understanding, and of stimulating correct
judgment and decision in New Testament ethics (various aspects of redaction criticism will be much in
play here).

Under the third group lays the study of particular
ethical topics of problems which may be present or referred
to in one of more new Testament works. Such topics are
the familiar ethical problems such as pacifism and nonviolence; church and state/religion and politics;

authority; eschatology and the problem of interim ethics;
an ethic of love vs. an ethic of command; the various
aspects of personal, sexual, family and social morality.
Apart from attempting to treat Christian biblical ethics
as a whole, such topics are probably the most difficult
for an exegete to handle to the satisfaction of colleagues
from outside biblical scholarship. For such investigations involve the biblical scholar most heavily precisely
in those aspects of the hermeneutical and methodological
circles which are least patient of objective control. A
reliable job on a particular ethical topic which crops
up in several places in the New Testament requires a fairly
good control of the whole picture of Christian biblical
ethics. For the picture or impression of the whole which
a scholar has inevitably influences how he finds, interprets, judges and takes a stand regarding the data. Errors
and inadequacies in one's foundational overview, or even
just the particular qualities it may have, inevitably
affect one's results. And yet, as complex as this may
be, it is still relatively simple when compared with the
problem of trying to sort out results which have come from
differing, even opposing foundational overviews.

All of this can help give some idea why so much time
has been spent attempting to spell out my foundational
overview, and why this paper is called "*Towards* a Christian Biblical Ethics." The actual work of the project has
hardly even begun. But such an overview, as difficult
as it is to formulate, seems to be a necessary precon-
dition for having some critical control over the manner
in which presuppositions influence research and conclusions. On the other hand, since it is obviously unreason-
able to expect everyone to go through such a laborious

process, the overview presented here may meet with enough agreement to make possible teamwork or task force divisions and subdivisions of the whole project.

Whether by this means the dream of developing an integral, fully operational Christian biblical ethic will be realized is perhaps not the best way to put the question. Paradise is not for this life either. But every significant step closer to the fulfillment of this dream is itself a victory. For each step closer will bring something that alone, individual scholars could not have achieved. A second happy product will be developing habits of collegial cooperation, and perhaps even a methodological model, which might prove useful in other areas as well.

Notes

[1]This essay represents my fifth effort to present
this topic. All four previous versions have been subjected
to fairly extensive discussion and critique: as continuing seminars at the 1975 and 1976 Catholic Biblical Association general meetings, as the topic of discussion at
the November 1975 and February 1977 meetings of the Boston Theological Society, as the subject of two sessions
of the faculty-student seminars of the Boston College--
Andover Newton Theological School Joint Doctoral Program,
and most recently with the scripture working group of the
1977 annual convention of the College Theology Society.
Also, the discussion group on this subject led by Lisa
Cahill at the June 1977 annual meeting of the Catholic
Theological Society of America was very useful. Now that
the program committee for the general meeting of the CBA
has given the project of studying a method for doing New
Testament ethics the status of a task force, I am hope-
ful that the topic will receive additional attention.

[2]By "New Testament ethics," therefore, is meant biblical ethics done from the specifically Christian perspective which sees the books of the New Testament as
having been profoundly influenced by the Old Testament and
post-biblical Judaism, as well as by the Christian faith
communities which produced them.

[3]For an example of how inadequate the ethics of Paul
or John are for our purposes, see Jack T. Sanders, *Ethics
in the New Testament* (Philadelphia: Fortress Press, 1975),
pp. 99-100

[4]From a section entitled "The Unity of NT Ethics"

in H. D. Wendland, *Ethik des Neuen Testaments* (NTD Ergänzungsreihe 4; Göttingen: Vandenhoeck und Ruprecht, 1970), pp. 122-24.

[5]Cf. B. Birch and L. Rasmussen, *Bible and Ethics in the Christian Life* (Minneapolis: Augsburg, 1976). This book provides an excellent up-to-date summary of recent American scholarship on this question.

[6]J. Gustafson, *Can Ethics Be Christian?* (Chicago: University of Chicago Press, 1975), see esp. pp. 146-61. Note that the inadequacy in Gustafson's approach is certainly due in large measure to the fact that in this book he poses the question from outside the Christian "conspiracy." His *Christ and the Moral Life* (New York: Harper & Row, 1968) would indicate that our positions are much closer than they seem to be in this discussion.

[7]Cf. Birch and Rasmussen, *op. cit.*, see esp. pp. 80-94. The works of Stanley Hauerwas in character and virtue, Walter Conn in moral development, and James W. Fowler III in faith development are well known. Among the moral philosophers, William Frankena, Lawrence Becker and Philippa Foot should be mentioned.

[8]I am not, of course, rejecting Chalcedonian Christology when I seem to speak of Jesus as a human person.

[9]Ignorance of world religions causes the author to try to refrain from discussing the relationship between Christian faith ethics and non-Christian faith ethics.

[10]R. Coste, "Pacifism and Legitimate Defense," *Concilium* 5 (1965), p. 87.

[11]I align myself closely to the position outlined by Joachim Jeremias, *The Problem of the Historical Jesus*

(Philadelphia: Fortress Press, 1964).

[12]Cf. H. -G. Gadamer, *Truth and Method* (New York: Seabury, 1975) and F. Lawrence, "The Hermeneutical Circle in Gadamer and Lonergan" (Dissertation, Basel, 1976).

[13]Cf. B. Lonergan, *Method in Theology* (London and New York: Herder & Herder, 1972), p. xi and passim; E. Fortin, "Thoughts on Modernity" in *Conditions and Purposes of the Modern University: The Christian Dimension* (Washington, D.C.: The Catholic Commission on Intellectual and Cultural Affairs, 1965), pp. 19-30.

[14]I am indebted to my colleague, Frederick Lawrence, for many of the insights of this section.

[15]As biblical scholars well know, parable research and literary research into biblical narratives has had a flowering in the past few years. Much of what is said here has been proximately stimulated by remarks of Paul Ricoeur: "Listening to the Parables of Jesus," *Criterion* 3 (1974), pp. 18-22. Cf. also his "Manifestation and Proclamation," *Archivio di Filosofia,* Enrico Castelli, dir. (Padova, 1974), pp. 57-76.

CONTRIBUTORS

Robert J. Daly, S.J. chairman of the Department of Theology at Boston College, has recently published his extensive study on Christian sacrifice.

Elizabeth Schüssler Fiorenza is associate professor of New Testament studies at the University of Notre Dame and has written much on the role of women in the church.

Reginald H. Fuller, whose works on New Testament Christology and the resurrection narratives are widely known, is presently Professor of New Testament at the Protestant Episcopal Seminary of Virginia.

Geffrey B. Kelly is associate professor of Religion at La Salle College, Philadelphia, Pa., and national secretary of the Bonhoeffer Society.

James P. Mackey, professor of systematic theology at the University of San Francisco, has authored many articles on the relationship of Christian faith and critical history.

Wayne A. Meeks who has in recent years devoted much of his research to the social history of early Christianity is professor of Religious Studies at Yale University.

Paul Misner has written several studies on 19th-century theology as a member of the American Academy of Religion Task Force on 19th-century Christian studies.

Thomas J. Ryan is associate professor of Theology at St. Joseph's College, Philadelphia, Pa.

Gerard S. Sloyan is professor of New Testament at Temple University and author of *Jesus on Trial*.